FR. LUIGI FACCENDA, O.F.M. CONV.

One More Gift

*Total Consecration to the Immaculata
According to the Spirituality of
Saint Maximilian Kolbe*

IMMACULATA PRESS
WEST COVINA, CALIFORNIA

Translation from selected writings and homilies in
Italian of Fr. Luigi Faccenda, O.F.M. Conv.
by the Father Kolbe Missionaries of the Immaculata

Italian originals:
Era Mariana (1980), *Ora tocca a voi* (1989)
© Edizioni dell'Immacolata, Bologna, Italy

© 1990 Immaculata Press
531 East Merced Avenue
West Covina, California 91790
(818) 917–0040
Second printing 1991
ISBN 0–96259–530–6
Library of Congress catalog number 90–81421
Printed in the United States of America

Contents

Foreword

St. Maximilian Kolbe, in the year of his death, posed to the Blessed Virgin Mary a question: "Who are you, O Immaculate Conception?" Her response inflamed his soul with steadfast hope that issued into love amidst the trials of war-torn Poland. Inspired by the example of this Marian martyr of Auschwitz, an Italian Franciscan would pose the same question to Our Lady thirteen years later. Fr. Luigi Faccenda, O.F.M. Conv. would likewise discover in the person of Mary Immaculate a sign of hope for himself and for others. Appropriately the Secular Institute of consecrated women that Fr. Luigi founded in 1954 links the two names of Our Lady and St. Maximilian: "Fr. Kolbe Missionaries of the Immaculata." Through this Institute, Fr. Luigi hoped, the world would be able to see in a visible way and collective form, the answer to the question that he and St. Maximilian had posed: "Who are you, O Immaculate Conception?"

Since its foundation, the Institute of the Fr. Kolbe Missionaries of the Immaculata has made the publishing apostolate a major component of its evangelization work. Among the books it has published are numbered over twenty titles by Fr. Luigi Faccenda himself. In the past thirty-five years, Fr. Luigi has become one of Italy's most inspired and prolific religious writers. In a personalist fashion, not unlike his mentor St. Maximilian, Fr. Luigi integrates a Marian theology and spirituality, and gives to both a pastoral application. His works have spanned the era of the Second Vatican Council, bridging pre-conciliar preparatory concerns and post-conciliar follow-up. One timeless theme runs consistently through all of his writings: Mary is Our Hope ("Spes Nostra"). Vatican II depicted Mary as "a sign of sure hope and solace for the pilgrim People of God" (LG 68). The Fr. Kolbe Missionaries of the Immaculata salute her as such in their Institute's motto: "Spes Nostra, Salve."

In *One More Gift*, the English-speaking world is being treated to the first major translation of materials from the corpus of Fr. Luigi Faccenda's writings. In this volume, Fr. Luigi indicates how Jesus' gift of Mary to us on Calvary can be reciprocated through our gift of self to Him through Mary. United with Mary, through a bond of personal consecration to the Immaculata, people can come into God's loving presence as matching gifts of love—identified with the Immaculata as "other Marys" and thereby all the more pleasing in God's sight.

One More Gift moves from a consideration of the theological basis for Marian consecration, through an historical and analytical exposition of its spiritual dynamism, to a challenging depiction of its missionary implications for an active Christian in the contemporary Church. St. Maximilian Kolbe emerges in this treatment as the Twentieth Century's teacher *par excellence* of consecration to Mary in its role as a powerful catalyst of the spiritual and apostolic life.

When I first met Fr. Luigi Faccenda in Bologna, Italy, several years ago, I was not surprised to discover that he has serenely borne the cross of suffering and infirmity for nearly as many years as he has been preaching and writing about the consecration to Mary. The ultimate stamp of authenticity on one's spiritual and apostolic life is the grace of "suffering willed out of love." St. Maximilian Kolbe's martyrdom at Auschwitz verified a desire for "love unto victimhood" that the saint had expressed years earlier as a young priest in Rome. One might say that St. Maximilian's *red* martyrdom in the concentration camp gave an authentication to his *white* martyrdom of daily life poured out, through Marian consecration, in self-sacrificing love for the Church. I suspect that Fr. Luigi Faccenda's teaching about the white martyrdom of Marian consecration derives its potency from his own life's sufferings. May all who read *One More Gift* find in the words and example of St. Maximilian Kolbe the same challenge of self-giving love that continues to animate its author.

At Cana, Mary challenged the waiters: "Do whatever he tells you" (Jn 2:5). Eventually Jesus does in fact *tell* us the "bottom line": "Greater love than this no one has, that one lay down his life for his friends" (Jn 15:13). Fr. Luigi Faccenda presents Mary to us in Kolbean fashion as our greatest help in acquiring that "no greater love," and thereby doing what Jesus tells us. May *One More Gift* help us understand and respond wholeheartedly to this Gospel challenge.

Fr. James E. McCurry, O.F.M. Conv.

National Director of the Militia Immaculatae Movement in the United States of America

Abbreviations

LG   *Lumen Gentium*, Dogmatic Constitution on the Church, Vatican Council II (1964).

MC   *Marialis Cultus*, Apostolic Exhortation of Pope Paul VI for the Right Ordering and Development of Devotion to the Blessed Virgin Mary (1974).

RM   *Redemptoris Mater*, Encyclical Letter of Pope John Paul II on the Blessed Virgin Mary in the Life of the Pilgrim Church (1987).

Conf.   Conferences and talks given by St. Maximilian Kolbe and summarized by Brothers who heard them.

Sketch Material written by St. Maximilian Kolbe which he was collecting for a book.

SK   Reference to the Italian edition of Kolbe's writings: *Gli Scritti di Massimiliano Kolbe, Eroe di Oświęcim e Beato della Chiesa,*

translation from Polish by Cristoforo
Zambelli, 3 vols. (Florence, Italy, Cittá
di Vita, 1976–78). The number will be
the text designation assigned by the
Polish and Italian editors.

Introduction

At the beginning of my religious life, St. Maximilian Kolbe led me in the footsteps of Mary. He showed me the consecration to the Immaculata as the greatest help in being faithful to the voice of the Lord and in serving the Church and mankind.

For this reason I have spent my entire life and I will spend my last energies making her known and loved by all my brethren.

I firmly believe that all of us, following her example, trusting in her intercession, and consecrating ourselves totally to her Immaculate Heart, will be led to rediscover the true face of Christ, of the Church, and our true dignity as children of God. We will be led to overcome any temptation and to be generous witnesses of our Faith in the world.

With this trust, I share with you some reflections on consecration to the Immaculata according to the spirituality of St. Maximilian Kolbe.

May the Holy Spirit enlighten you to penetrate the richness of this "One More Gift" which Jesus gave us on Calvary when He said, "Behold your mother!"

Fr. Luigi Faccenda, O.F.M. Conv.

St. Maximilian Kolbe, Apostle of Mary and Martyr of Charity.

Biographical Note on St. Maximilian Kolbe

(by Pope Paul VI)

Who is Maximilian Kolbe? You know the answer; you know him well. So close is he to our generation, to the happenings we have all experienced in our time, that we all know about him. Few other processes of beatification have been conducted amidst such a wealth of information. Solely because we wish to show ourselves concerned with historical truth today, we shall present first of all a biographical sketch of Father Kolbe, written by someone who has studied him very carefully.

The Life of the New Blessed

Father Maximilian Kolbe was born at Zduńska Wola, near Lodz, on January 8, 1894. In 1907 he entered the seminary of the Friars Minor Conventual, and later was sent to Rome where he continued his ecclesiastical studies at the Pontifical Gregorian University and at the Franciscan Seraphicum. While still a student he founded the *Militia Immaculatae*. After his ordination on April 28, 1918 he returned to Poland and initiated his Marian apostolate, launching a monthly review, *The Knight of the Immaculata*, which by 1938 reached a circulation of nearly a million.

In 1927 he founded Niepokalanów, "the City of the Immaculata," a center for religious life and for various types of apostolate. In 1930 he set out for Japan, where he established a similar center. After returning permanently to Poland, he dedicated himself entirely to the task of publishing various religious periodicals. The Second World War found him at the head of the biggest publishing concern in Poland. On September 19, 1939, he was arrested by the Gestapo and deported first to Lamsdorf, Germany, and then to the concentration camp of Amtitz. Released on December 8, 1939, he returned to Niepokalanów, and took up anew his interrupted activities. Arrested again in 1941, he was incarcerated in the prison of Pawiak, at Warsaw, then sent off to the concentration camp at Oświęcim (Auschwitz). Having offered to take the place of an unknown fellow prisoner who had been condemned to death in reprisal for the escape of another prisoner, he was consigned to a bunker there to die of starvation. On August 14, 1941, he was put to death by being given an injection of poison. It was the eve of the Assumption. Thus did he yield up his beautiful soul to God, after having helped and consoled his fellow sufferers. His body, like theirs, was burnt (Fr. Ernesto Piacentini, O.F.M. Conv.).

His Veneration of the Immaculate Conception

Maximilian Kolbe was an apostle of the formal veneration of Mary seen in all her pristine splendor, in the original and privileged character of the definition she gave of herself at Lourdes: the Immaculate Conception. It is impossible to separate the name of Father Kolbe, his activity or his mission, from the name of Mary Immaculate. He founded the *Militia Immaculatae* here in Rome before he was even a priest, on October 16, 1917; . . . We all know how this humble, meek Franciscan, with incredible courage and extraordinary talent for organization, developed this initiative of his, and made of the devotion to the Mother of Christ, the Woman clothed with the sun, the center of his spirituality, his apostolate, and his theology. Let us not be reluctant to admire him, to adopt the watchword which the new Blessed leaves us as his legacy, as though we feared that such zeal to honor Mary might clash with the other two theological and spiritual currents so prominent in today's religious thought and life: the Christological trend, and the ecclesiological trend. No competition here! In Father

Kolbe's mind, Christ occupies not merely the first place, but strictly speaking, the only place necessary and sufficient for salvation. Nor is love for the Church and for her mission absent from the teaching or the apostolic endeavors of our new Blessed. For it is precisely from the way Mary completes and serves the universal plan of Christ for the salvation of all men that she draws all her prerogatives and all her greatness.[1]

Notes

Fr. Maximilian Kolbe was canonized by Pope John Paul II on October 10, 1982.

[1] Pope Paul VI, *Discourse at Maximilian Kolbe's Beatification* (October 17, 1971).

Chapter One

Total Consecration to the Immaculata: Theological Basis

Mary's Maternal Mediation

In order to understand well the meaning of total consecration to Mary, it is necessary to think of Mary's mission as Mediatrix in the plan of redemption.

The Second Vatican Council confers on her the title of *Mediatrix*, understood, of course, as dependent on the unique mediation of Jesus Christ.

The Dogmatic Constitution on the Church *Lumen Gentium* states:

> The Blessed Virgin is invoked in the Church under the titles of Advocate, Helper, Benefactress, and Mediatrix. This, however, is so understood that it neither takes away anything from nor adds anything to the dignity and efficacy of Christ the one Mediator. No creature could ever be counted along with the Incarnate Word and Redeemer; but just as the priesthood of Christ is shared in various ways both by his ministers and the faithful, and as the one good-

ness of God is radiated in different ways among his creatures, so also the unique mediation of the Redeemer does not exclude but rather gives rise to a manifold cooperation which is but a sharing in this one source.

The Church does not hesitate to profess this subordinate role of Mary, which she constantly experiences and recommends to the heartfelt attention of the faithful, so that encouraged by this maternal help they may the more closely adhere to the Mediator and Redeemer.[1]

In this text the precise meaning of Mary's mediation is expressed. Chapter VIII of this document is the first document in the Church's history which explains this idea so clearly.

Mary's Mediation in the History of the Church

The idea of Mary's mediation is found at the beginning of the Third Century in one of the oldest Marian prayers *Sub tuum praesidium*. ("We fly to your patronage, O Holy Mother of God; despise not our petitions in our necessities, but deliver us always from all dangers, O glorious and Blessed Virgin.")

In the Fourth Century St. Ephrem (the first "singer of Mary") without hesitation invoked her as *Mediatrix* (cf. RM 31).

The Council of Ephesus, in 431, began to clarify the true dimensions of Mary's role toward mankind.

Andrew of Crete, who died in 740, addressed

Our Lady with the following invocation, "When you leave us for God, we gain in you a Mediatrix."

St. Bernard, in the Twelfth Century, emphasized Mary's role as Mediatrix between Christ and the Church as the *aqueduct* through which all graces flow. St. Bernard in one of his homilies expressed his profound love for the Mediatrix of all graces:

When you find yourself tossed by the raging storms on this great sea of life, far from land, keep your eyes fixed on this Star to avoid disaster. When the winds of temptation or the rocks of tribulation threaten, look up to the Star, call upon Mary! When the waves of pride or ambition sweep over you, when the tide of detraction or jealousy runs against you, look up to the Star, call upon Mary! When the shipwreck of avarice, anger, or lust seems imminent, call upon Mary!

If the horror of sin overwhelms you and the voice of conscience terrifies you, if the fear of judgment, the abyss of sadness, and the depths of despair clutch at your heart, think of Mary! In dangers, difficulties and doubts, think about Mary, call upon Mary! Keep her name on your lips, her love in your heart. Imitate her and her powerful intercession will surround you. Following her, you will not stray. Praying to her, you will ward off disaster and despair. Meditate about her and you will not err. Cling to her and you cannot fall.

With her protection, there is nothing to fear.
Under her leadership, you will succeed. With
her encouragement, all is possible.[2]

From the Middle Ages to the present, Mary's title
of Mediatrix appears in many different expressions.

Pius IX was the first Pope who addressed the
Immaculate Mother of God under the title of "Most
powerful Mediatrix and Reconciler of the whole
world with her only begotten Son, most radiant
beauty and ornament of the Church and its strongest
defense."[3]

Leo XIII in similar definitions called her Co-
Redemptrix. "It may be affirmed . . . with truth
and precision that, by the will of God, absolutely no
part of that immense treasure of every grace which
the Lord amasses . . . is bestowed on us except
through Mary."[4]

"She is the one of whom Jesus was born. She is
his true Mother and for this reason a worthy and
acceptable Mediatrix to the Mediator."[5]

St. Pius X wrote: "It was given to the Sacred
Virgin to become the most powerful Mediatrix and
Conciliatrix of the whole earth with her only be-
gotten Son."[6]

The Popes Benedict XV and Pius XI attributed to
the Blessed Virgin the title of true Co-Redemptrix.

Pius XII in his Encyclical Letters *Mystici Corporis*
(1943) and *Haurietis Aquas* (1956) confirmed the
teaching of his predecessors. He took from the
riches of the Church's tradition the valid motive for
calling the faithful to nourish an unlimited confi-

dence in the mediation of the Virgin Co-Redemptrix. In his document *Quamvis Plane* he stated: " Near the throne of the Most High we have the most clement Mother of God and our Mother who, by her powerful intercession, surely can obtain everything for us. Let us, then, entrust ourselves and all that belongs to us to her patronage."

Paul VI in his Apostolic Exhortation *Marialis Cultus* answered the questions why and how Mary must enter into Christian life. He proclaimed that we are to consecrate ourselves to her:

> Christ is the only way to the Father (cf. Jn 14:4–11) and the ultimate example to whom the disciple must conform his own conduct (cf. Jn 13:15), to the extent of sharing Christ's sentiments (cf. Phil 2:5), living his life and possessing his Spirit (cf. Gal 2:20; Rom 8:10–11). The Church has always taught this and nothing in pastoral activity should obscure this doctrine. But the Church, taught by the Holy Spirit and benefitting from centuries of experience, recognizes that devotion to the Blessed Virgin, subordinated to worship of the divine Savior, and in connection with it, also has a great pastoral effectiveness and constitutes a force for renewing Christian living. It is easy to see the reason for this effectiveness.[7]

Recently, Pope John Paul II in his Marian Encyclical *Redemptoris Mater* stressed the significance of Mary's maternal mediation.

Mary's mediation *is intimately linked with her motherhood*. It possesses a specifically maternal character, which distinguishes it from the mediation of the other creatures who in various and always subordinate ways share in the one mediation of Christ, although her own mediation is also a shared mediation . . . *"a sharing in the one unique source that is the mediation of Christ Himself."* . . . This role [of Mary] is at the same time *special and extraordinary*. . . . This role constitutes a real dimension of her presence in the saving mystery of Christ and the Church.[8]

We can conclude that the Blessed Virgin as a true Queen of grace and mercy, taken up into heavenly glory, distributes the spiritual treasures won by her Son during his life on earth from the Incarnation to the immolation on Calvary.

The entire people of God gratefully invoke, venerate, and love her as the Help of Christians, the Benefactress and Consoler, the Dispenser of all graces, and the Queen of grace and mercy.

Notes

[1] Vatican Council II, Dogmatic Constitution on the Church *Lumen Gentium* (1964), 62.

[2] St. Bernard, *Super Missus Est*, Homilia II, 17.

[3] Pope Pius IX, Apostolic Constitution Defining the Dogma of the Immaculate Conception *Ineffabilis Deus* (December 8, 1854).

[4] Pope Leo XIII, Encyclical Letter on the Rosary *Octobri Mense* (September 22, 1891).

[5] Pope Leo XIII, Encyclical Letter on the Rosary *Fidentem Piumque* (September 20, 1896).

[6] St. Pius X, Encyclical Letter on the Fiftieth Anniversary of the Definition of the Dogma of the Immaculate Conception *Ad Diem Illum* (February 2, 1904).

[7] Pope Paul VI, Apostolic Exhortation for the Right Ordering and Development of Devotion to the Blessed Virgin Mary *Marialis Cultus* (February 2, 1974), 57.

[8] Pope John Paul II, Encyclical Letter on the Blessed Virgin Mary in the Life of the Pilgrim Church *Redemptoris Mater* (March 25, 1987), 38.

Chapter Two

Consecration in the Church's Tradition

John Damascene, in the Eighth Century, already spoke about consecration to Mary:

> Today, we too, do linger in your presence,
> O Sovereign! I say again:
> Sovereign, Virgin Mother of God,
> and let us bind our souls,
> as to a steadfast and immovable anchor:
> to the hope that you are for us.
> Let us consecrate to you our spirit and soul,
> our body, our whole person.
> We wish to honor you,
> as far as we are able,
> with psalms, hymns, and spiritual songs. . . .[1]

However, it was not until the Seventeenth Century that the doctrine of Marian consecration developed with the "École Française" (French School): Bérulle, Olier, Douden, and above all, St. Louis Grignon de Montfort. In St. Louis' treatise *True Devotion to the Blessed Virgin*, we read:

The Father gave and still gives his Son only through her. He dispenses his graces to us only through her. God the Son was prepared for mankind in general by her alone. Mary, in union with the Holy Spirit, still conceives Him and brings Him forth daily. It is through her alone that the Son distributes his merits and virtues. The Holy Spirit formed Jesus only through her, and He forms the members of the Mystical Body and dispenses his gifts and his favors through her.

With such a compelling example of the three divine Persons before us, we would be extremely perverse to ignore her and not consecrate ourselves to her. Indeed we would be blind if we did not see the need for Mary in approaching God and making our total offering to Him.[2]

In 1891 the Bishops of Milan and Turin (Italy) promoted the consecration of all dioceses of the world to Mary.

At the beginning of the Twentieth Century in France, many asked for the consecration of all mankind. On October 21, 1942, Pope Pius XII, to commemorate the 25th anniversary of Fatima's apparitions, with the authority of his universal paternity, consecrated the Church and mankind to the Immaculate Heart of Mary: "To your Immaculate Heart, I, as universal father of the great Christian family, in this tragic hour of human history, entrust, submit, and consecrate not only the Church, the

Mystical Body of your Jesus . . . but also the whole
world, tormented by savage discords, parched by a
fire of hatred, and victimized by its own iniquities."

On September 13, 1959, the Conference of Italian
Bishops consecrated Italy to the Immaculate Heart
of Mary.

Pope Paul VI, on November 21, 1964, after having
proclaimed Mary as Mother of the Church, con-
cluded his hymn of praise and abandonment in
Mary by consecrating the whole human family to
her, with all its problems and trials, its legitimate
aspirations and ardent hopes.

In the Apostolic Exhortation *Signum Magnum* of
May 1967, Paul VI exhorted the people of God to
imitate Mary's virtues and recalled the consecration
of mankind by Pius XII and added:

> We exhort all the sons and daughters of the
> Church to renew personally their consecration
> to the Immaculate Heart of the Mother of the
> Church, and to bring alive this most noble act
> of veneration by a life ever more consonant
> with the divine will and in a spirit of filial
> service and of a devout imitation of their
> heavenly Queen.[3]

On January 26, 1979, Pope John Paul II, while
opening the Conference of Latin-American Bishops
in Mexico, pronounced the following prayer: "We
offer to you, O Mary, this people of God. We offer
to you the Church in Mexico and in the whole con-
tinent as your own possession. Make these hearts

worthy to be your dwelling place . . . we wish to put into your hands our entire future and the future of the evangelization in Latin America."

At Jasna Gora, during the Holy Father's journey to Poland, his expressions of love for the Immaculata became ever more frequent and fervent. On June 6, 1979, Pope John Paul II renewed his consecration to the Blessed Mother and with unlimited confidence entrusted the whole Church to her until the end of the world.

During the Jubilee Year of Redemption, on the Solemnity of the Annunciation, March 25, 1984, in union with all the bishops throughout the world, he pronounced the Solemn Act of Entrustment of the entire Church and humanity to her.

Our Holy Father, whose motto is *"Totus Tuus,"* (I am all Yours) not only consecrated his pontificate to Mary but also consecrates every nation which he visits to her. On September 16, 1987, during his second pastoral visit to the United States, he addressed Mary, Patroness of the United States of America under the title of her Immaculate Conception, with a special prayer of consecration:

I entrust to you, Virgin Mother of God, all the faithful of this land. I entrust to you all the people of God—the pilgrim People of God— called to be mindful of their Christian dignity, called to conversion, called to eternal life. . . . I ask you to strengthen the Catholic people in truth and love, in their obedience to the Commandments of God, and in their fidelity to the sacraments.

Virgin Mother of God, Our Lady of the Angels: I entrust to you the whole Church in America. Help her to excel in sacrifice and service. Purify her love, renew her life, and convert her constantly to the Gospel of your Son.

Lead her children with all their Christian brethren to eternal life, for the glory of your Son Jesus Christ, who lives and reigns with the Father in the unity of the Holy Spirit for ever and ever.[4]

In the Encyclical written on the occasion of the Marian Year, 1987/1988, Pope John Paul II presented the entrustment or consecration to Our Lady as the natural consequence of her mission in the plan of salvation as our Mother.

Of the essence of motherhood is the fact that it concerns the person. Motherhood always establishes a *unique and unrepeatable relationship between two people: between mother and child and between child and mother*.

Even when the same woman is the mother of many children, her personal relationship with each one of them is of the very essence of motherhood. . . .

It can be said that motherhood "in the order of grace" preserves the analogy with what "in the order of nature" characterizes the union between mother and child. In the light of this fact it becomes easier to understand why in Christ's testament his Mother's new motherhood is expressed in the singular, in reference to one man: "Behold your son."

It can also be said that these same words fully show the reason *for the Marian dimension of the life of Christ's disciples*. This is true not only of John, who at that hour stood at the foot of the Cross together with his Master's Mother, but it is also true of every disciple of Christ, of every Christian. The Redeemer entrusts his Mother to the disciple, and at the same time he gives her to him as his Mother. Mary's motherhood, which becomes man's inheritance, is a gift: *a gift which Christ Himself makes* personally to every individual.

The Redeemer entrusts Mary to John because He entrusts John to Mary.

At the foot of the Cross there begins that special *entrusting of humanity to the Mother of Christ*, which in the history of the Church has been practiced and expressed in different ways. The same Apostle and Evangelist, after reporting the words addressed by Jesus on the Cross to his Mother and to himself, adds: "And from that hour the disciple took her to his own home" (Jn 19:27).

This statement certainly means that the role

of son was attributed to the disciple and that he assumed responsibility for the Mother of his beloved Master.

And since Mary was given as a mother to him personally, the statement indicates, even though indirectly, everything expressed by the intimate relationship of a child with its mother. And all of this can be included in the word "entrusting." Such entrusting is *the response* to a person's love, and in particular *to the love of a mother*.

The Marian dimension of the life of a disciple of Christ is expressed in a special way precisely through this filial entrusting to the Mother of Christ, which began with the testament of the Redeemer on Golgotha.

Entrusting himself to Mary in a filial manner, the Christian, like the Apostle John, "welcomes" the Mother of Christ "into his own home" and brings her into everything that makes up his inner life, that is to say into his human and Christian "I": he "*took her to his own home.*". . .

This filial relationship, this self-entrusting of a child to its mother, not only has its *beginning in Christ* but can also be said to be *definitively directed towards Him*. Mary can be said to continue to say to each individual the words which she spoke at Cana in Galilee: "Do whatever He tells you."[5]

Doctrinal Dimension

Consecration to the Immaculata is the natural consequence of the spiritual bonds which unite mankind to Mary in the plan of redemption. Mary is the Mother of Jesus and our Mother too. Through her we have received our Savior. She is our Co-Redemptrix, for on Calvary she associated herself with the sufferings of Christ efficaciously cooperating with Him in our redemption. By reason of her dignity as Mother of God and her mission as our Co-Redemptrix and Mediatrix of all graces, she received the right to absolute sovereignty after Jesus over all of us.

Therefore, we owe her our full homage and our total dedication.

According to the traditional definition, consecration to Mary consists in *"offering oneself entirely to Mary, in order, through her, to belong totally to Jesus."* This consecration implies a complete and never-ending dedication of ourselves to the Blessed Virgin (all that we are and have) and a generous and total dependence on her.

These two conditions (totality and perpetuity), which are indispensable for a perfect consecration, reach their highest degree and their highest expression in the offering to God suggested by the ascetic French writers of the Seventeenth Century (Bérulle, Olier, de Montfort).

St. Louis de Montfort presents Marian consecration as a special way of totally living our Baptism.

I have said that this devotion could rightly be called a perfect renewal of the vows and promises of holy Baptism. Before Baptism every Christian was a slave of the devil because he belonged to him. At Baptism he has either personally or through his sponsors solemnly renounced Satan, his seduction, and his works. He has chosen Jesus as his Master and sovereign Lord and undertaken to depend upon Him as a slave of love. This is what is done in the devotion I am presenting to you . . . as expressed in the act of consecration. . . .

We even do something more than at Baptism, when ordinarily our godparents speak for us and we are given to Jesus only by proxy.

In this devotion we give ourselves personally and freely and we are fully aware of what we are doing.[6]

Anthropological Dimension of Marian Consecration

After having meditated on the teaching of many saints, apostles, and doctors about consecration to Our Lady, I believe it is very useful to reflect on its anthropological dimension.

In fact, through our consecration we offer to Mary our soul with all its powers and faculties: affections, memory, intellect, will, and freedom. We offer to her our material goods, both present and future. We give her our spiritual goods which means our merits, virtues, and past, present, and future good works. This offering involves not only the goodness in us but also our sinfulness and weaknesses. The Heart of Mary is like an altar on which all that we are becomes like incense because she purifies and enriches it with her fullness of grace and her merits. Mary takes possession of our whole being, offering it to God as her own.

This consecration also includes our offering our body to Mary with its senses, powers, and needs. These ideas are quite concrete because they concern "the whole person," including his or her sexuality and generative power.

Marian consecration is a powerful means by which one can discover and live his or her vocation. One becomes Mary's possession and, at the same time, Jesus', by the unconditional and unlimited offering of oneself to the Immaculata. Therefore, the choices of celibacy, virginity, or family life acquire in Mary the infinite value of her love and Heart. If man and woman understand that consecration to Mary involves their whole being, they will not easily fall prey to feelings of frustration if called to the mystical marriage in religious life, the priesthood, or any other form of consecrated life (that is Secular Institutes) approved by the Church.

Through Mary's presence and action those who are called to form a family will be able to live conjugal love and experience the joy of parenthood according to God's will.

In this way one will not be afraid to give too

much importance to spiritual values and thus dis-
regard the body, or vice versa because we balance
our life with faith so as not to fall into naturalism.[7]
At the same time we can judge correctly those
feelings and psychological tensions which we perceive, even without often understanding their origins
and causes.

By this concept, which fully corresponds to the
essence of consecration, Catholics (young women
and men, religious, priests, married couples, everyone without distinction) will live their vocations in
God's plan of salvation. They will accomplish the
duties inherent in their state and condition of life
with the certitude that they are praising God and
working for the good of mankind. They will thus
live the fullness of their Baptism.

Consecration to Mary of
Priests and Consecrated Persons

Total consecration to the Immaculata is truly a
key for achieving sanctity for all Catholics because it
leads them to fulfill the commitments derived from
Baptism in maturity of faith. For any person consecrated to God it becomes almost a requirement
both for reaching one's own sanctification and for
making the apostolate fruitful.

Consecration to Mary becomes an antidote to
secularism,[8] for it recalls everything God worked in
the history of salvation. It reminds us that the gift of
Baptism incorporates us into Christ's mysteries and
into the salvific community of the Church.

The consecrated are supported in their priesthood or consecrated life (cf. LG 44) by the vigilant and maternal protection of Mary, the Mother, Teacher, and Model of the first Apostle and of the Twelve Apostles.

The Second Vatican Council and the Magisterium under Pope Paul VI taught the meaning and value of consecration to Mary with great clarity. Presently Pope John Paul II is bringing about a wave of renewal in the whole Church through his powerful love for Mary. He communicates this love by his example and his word to all he meets, especially consecrated persons and priests.

Speaking from the Cross on Golgotha, Christ said to the disciple: "Behold, your mother." And the disciple "took her to his own home" as Mother. *Let us also take Mary as Mother into the interior "home" of our Priesthood.* For we belong to the "faithful in whose rebirth and development" the Mother of God "cooperates with a maternal love." Yes, we have, in a certain sense, a special "right" to this love in consideration of the mystery of the Upper Room. Christ said: "No longer do I call you servants . . . , but I have called you friends" (Jn 15:15). . . .

Such a friendship involves a commitment. Such a friendship should instill a holy fear, a much greater sense of responsibility, a much greater readiness to give of oneself all that one can, with the help of God. . . .

We always feel unworthy of Christ's friendship. But it is a good thing that we should have a holy fear of not remaining faithful to it. The Mother of Christ knows all this. . . .

The Mother of God, who (as the Council teaches) cooperates, with a mother's love, in the rebirth and the training of all those who become brothers of her Son—who become his friends—will do everything in her power so that they may not betray this holy friendship, so that they may be worthy of it.[9]

"There is no greater love than this: to lay down one's life for one's friends" (Jn 15:13).

Pope John Paul II visits the starvation cell of Auschwitz where Fr. Kolbe died on August 14, 1941.

Notes

[1] St. John Damascene, *Homilia in Dormitionem*.

[2] St. Louis-Marie Grignon de Montfort, *Traité de la vraie dévotion à la sainte Vièrge*, 140. English trans. *True Devotion to the Blessed Virgin* (Bay Shore, New York: Montfort Publications, 1980).

[3] Pope Paul VI, Apostolic Exhortation on the Cult to the Blessed Virgin Mary Mother of the Church and Model of all Virtues *Signum Magnum*, (May 13, 1967), 8.

[4] Pope John Paul II, "Consecration to Mary", Los Angeles, California, September 16, 1987.

[5] Pope John Paul II, Encyclical Letter on the Blessed Virgin Mary in the Life of the Pilgrim Church *Redemptoris Mater* (March 25, 1987), 45–46.

[6] St. Louis-Marie Grignon de Montfort, *Traité de la vraie dévotion*, 126.

[7] Naturalism: action, inclination, or thought based only on natural desires and instincts; a theory denying that an event or object has a supernatural significance.

Naturalism is the view that the only reality that exists is nature, so that divine grace is either denied or ignored. There are two main forms. Philosophical naturalism claims that human beings were never elevated to a supernatural destiny; they will reach their final destiny by the sole use of their natural, individual, and social powers. Practical naturalism is human conduct that, by excluding prayer and the use of supernatural channels of grace, in effect says that the purpose of human existence is purely natural.

[8] Secularism: indifference to or rejection or exclusion of

religion and religious considerations.

It is a closed system that affirms that human existence and destiny are fully explainable in terms of this world without reference to eternity.

[9] Pope John Paul II, "Behold, Your Mother: Letter to Priests for Holy Thursday 1988" (Boston: St. Paul Books and Media, 1988).

Chapter Three

Theological Basis of Kolbean Spirituality

The Marian thought of Fr. Kolbe has an eminently doctrinal and pastoral orientation. He felt the immediacy of understanding the mystery of Mary and of sharing this knowledge with mankind.

He was convinced that a true knowledge and devotion to her would in turn give birth to a dynamic Christian life, even to the level of sanctity.

This can be called true Marian spirituality.

St. Maximilian Kolbe stated:

> When we reflect on these two truths: that all graces come from the Father by the Son and the Holy Spirit; and that our Holy Mother Mary is, so to speak, one with the Holy Spirit, we are driven to the conclusion that this Most Holy Mother is indeed the intermediary by whom all graces come to us. [1]
>
> In the union of the Holy Spirit with her, not only do we have the love of two beings; in one of the two we have all the love of the Trinity Itself; and in the other we have all creation's

love. Hence, in this union heaven and earth meet; all of heaven with all of earth, the totality of divine eternal love with the plenitude of created love. It is the true summit of love.[2]

In regards to Mary's mediation, Fr. Kolbe does not think of it as a passage from Mary to Christ in which the Blessed Virgin would impede direct contact between Christ and men. Mary's mediation is a passage *"with Mary to Christ."*

It may seem that Jesus is something different from Our Lady; that Jesus is one object and Our Lady the other; that if one turns to Our Lady for everything he honors Jesus too little. This is an erroneous understanding since Jesus is God incarnate in her. . . . We know perfectly well that the object of all devotion is God. In the same way, the cult offered to the Immaculata is a direct means to this end. We should search for Jesus through her and not in another place but only in her. We pass with her to the Other.[3]

This is why he can declare with certainty:

The Immaculata has left this earth, but her life has only grown the richer; and it develops and flourishes more and more in the lives of Christians. If all the souls that have lived on this earth, and all those that still struggle here could make known the all-powerful influence the Immaculata has exercised on them, and her maternal solicitude for these souls redeemed by the precious Blood of her Son, what an incalculable number of volumes would be required! All these people recount only what they had been able to discover as special graces received through Mary. But in fact every grace that comes to a soul comes from her hands, for she is the Mediatrix of all graces; and at every moment new graces penetrate into the souls of men. There are graces which enlighten the intellect, which strengthen the will, which draw us towards what is good. There are ordinary and extraordinary graces; some directly concern our natural life, while others have to do with the sanctification of our souls. Only at the Last Judgment, only in heaven will we discover with what loving attention our heavenly Mother watched over each one of us without ceasing, over every soul individually, because all are her children. She strives to shape them after the model of Jesus, her First-born, the archetype of all sanctity, the Man–God.[4]

Fr. Kolbe's thought is contained in this letter addressed to one of his brothers who questioned Mary's mediation and distribution of all graces:

The union between the Immaculata and the Holy Spirit is so inexpressible, yet so perfect that the Holy Spirit acts only by the Immaculata, his Spouse. This is why she is the Mediatrix of all graces given by the Holy Spirit. And since every grace is a gift of God the Father through the Son and by the Holy Spirit, it follows that there is no grace which Mary cannot dispose of as her own and which is not given to her for this purpose.[5]

Since Mary is the only way to sanctity, Fr. Kolbe teaches we must belong ever more to her, and in and through her, to Jesus and to God the Father.

Pope Paul VI, in his homily at the beatification of Fr. Kolbe, ratified this doctrine when he affirmed:

> Kolbe, in accord with the whole of Catholic doctrine, the whole liturgy, and the entire theology of the interior life, sees Mary included in God's plan of salvation as the "term fixed by eternal counsel," as the woman filled with grace, as the Seat of Wisdom, as the woman destined from eternity to be the Mother of Christ, as the Queen of the Messianic Kingdom, and at the same time as the Handmaid of the Lord, chosen to participate in the redemptive act as Mother of the God–Man, our Savior. *"Mary is the one through whose intercession men reach Jesus and the one through whom Jesus reaches men."*[6]

Pope Paul VI, confirming Kolbe's Marian spirituality, added:

> Therefore our Blessed [Kolbe] is not to be reproved, nor the Church with him, because of their enthusiasm for the formal religious veneration of the Mother of God. This veneration with its rites and practices will never fully

achieve the level it merits, nor the benefits it can bring precisely because of the mystery that unites her to Christ, and which finds fascinating documentation in the New Testament. The result will never be a "Mariolatry," just as the sun will never be darkened by the moon; nor will the mission of salvation specifically entrusted to the ministry of the Church ever be distorted if the latter honors in Mary an exceptional Daughter and a spiritual Mother. The characteristic aspect, if you like, and the original quality of Blessed Kolbe's devotion, of his "hyperdulia"[7] to Mary, is the importance he attributes to it with regard to the present needs of the Church, the efficacy of her prophecy about the glory of the Lord and the vindication of the humble, the power of her intercession, the splendor of her exemplariness, the presence of her maternal charity. The Council confirmed us in these certainties, and now from Heaven Father Kolbe is teaching us and helping us to meditate upon them and live them.[8]

He ends with this final praise:

This Marian profile of our new Blessed places him among the great saints and the seers who have understood, venerated, and sung the mystery of Mary.[9]

St. Louis de Montfort
and St. Maximilian Kolbe

Total consecration to Our Lady may be expressed in many different forms and can be understood, explained, and lived in many different ways although the doctrinal basis and the substance are the same.

What the Holy Father Pius XII uttered in his discourse on the occasion of St. Louis de Montfort's canonization is truly significant:

> True devotion, traditional devotion, that of the Church, the devotion, we might say, of the good-intentioned Christian and Catholic, aims essentially at union with Jesus under the guidance of Mary. The form and practice of this devotion may vary according to time, place, and personal inclination. Within the bounds of sound and safe doctrine, of orthodoxy and dignity of worship, the Church leaves her children a just margin of liberty. She is conscious that true and perfect devotion to Our Lady is not bound up in any particular modes in such a way that one of them can claim a monopoly over the others. [10]

Hence, it is true that the different forms of consecration to Mary do not exclude but complement one another because each one of them expresses certain aspects and characteristics of the same fundamental doctrine.

The purpose of this work is to treat the subject of total consecration in Kolbean spirituality. Yet, before we delve into his thought, it is appropriate that we recognize the great Marian apostle, St. Louis Grignon de Montfort, who preceded St. Maximilian Kolbe (as we have seen in the second chapter). His treatise *True Devotion* is an incomparable systematic doctrinal work of which Fr. Kolbe spoke with enthusiasm (cf. SK 282 and 508).

Frater Paul Moratti, one of Kolbe's more intimate disciples, affirmed that he knew St. Louis de Montfort through St. Maximilian. It is also known that the rector of the Seraphic College in Rome, during the final years of St. Maximilian's ecclesiastical studies, was Fr. Stephen Ignudi, an ardent follower of de Montfort.

St. Grignon de Montfort and Kolbe are two original and unique personalities.

Though they deeply converge in conceiving the consecration as a "total self-giving to Mary," they have very different ways of presenting this total offering and its goals because of their different historical, cultural, and spiritual backgrounds.

We can affirm that there is a complementary originality between the two Saints' doctrines of consecration to Mary.[11]

Kolbe emphasized consecration to Mary as the Immaculate Conception and gave it a specific apostolic purpose: to gain the whole world for the Immaculata so as to bring about, as soon as possible, the kingdom of the Sacred Heart of Jesus (cf. SK 22).

The main factors which had an important influence in Kolbe's spirituality can be summarized in the following points:

a. The Franciscan school: its spirituality, its secular tradition of extraordinary veneration for the Immaculate Conception, its missionary ardor, and its universality.

b. The recent events which increased the Marian cult: the apparitions of St. Catherine Labouré (the Miraculous Medal) and Lourdes.

c. The religious atmosphere of Kolbe's time which encouraged Catholics to dedicate themselves more generously to the social apostolate.

d. Finally, his interior experiences and aspirations to become the greatest possible saint and to reach limitless horizons of love.

These factors, under the influence of divine grace, guided him to perceive, to undertake, and finally to fulfill his highest ideal of perfection.

His ideal, the orientation of his piety and Marian apostolate, and the characteristic form of his total consecration to the Immaculata can be defined with the following expression: *"to offer oneself to the Immaculata in a permanent state as a victim with apostolic intent."*

This spirituality gave birth to the *Militia Immaculatae* (MI), which he founded in 1917 while a student in Rome. It is a universal Marian movement with members from all walks of life who work for the Immaculata and with her for the evangelization and sanctification of the whole world.

Notes

[1] St. Maximilian Kolbe, Conference given September 25, 1937, *Immaculate Conception and the Holy Spirit: the Marian Teachings of Father Kolbe*, translated by Richard Arnandez, F.S.C. from materials compiled and translated by H. M. Manteau-Bonamy, O.P. (Kenosha, Wisconsin: Franciscan Marytown Press, 1977), 102.

[2] St. Maximilian Kolbe, Sketch, February 17, 1941 (SK 1318), *Immaculate Conception and the Holy Spirit*, 46–47.

[3] St. Maximilian Kolbe, Conf., April 25, 1937, *Panorama of the Marian Doctrine of Bl. Maximilian Kolbe*, translated by Most Rev. Donald Kos, O.F.M. Conv. from materials compiled and translated by Ernesto Piacentini, O.F.M. Conv. (Kenosha, Wisconsin: Franciscan Marytown Press, 1975), 37.

[4] St. Maximilian Kolbe, Sketch, August 1940 (SK 1313), *Immaculate Conception and the Holy Spirit*, 130.

[5] St. Maximilian Kolbe, Letter, July 28, 1935 (SK 634), *Immaculate Conception and the Holy Spirit*, 99.

[6] Pope Paul VI, *Discourse at Maximilian Kolbe's Beatification* (October 17, 1971).

[7] Hyperdulia: the special veneration due to the Blessed Virgin Mary. It is substantially less than the cultus "latria" (adoration), which is due to God alone. But it is higher than the cultus "dulia" (veneration), due to angels and other saints.

[8] Pope Paul VI, *Discourse at Maximilian Kolbe's Beatification* (October 17, 1971).

[9] Ibid.

[10] Pope Pius XII, *Audience on the Occasion of Louis de Montfort's Canonization* (July 21, 1947).

[11] Cf. Stefano De Fiores, S.M.M., "La Consacrazione all' Immacolata secondo P. Kolbe—Approccio Ermeneutico" in *La Mariologia di San Massimiliano M. Kolbe*, Atti del Congresso Internazionale Roma, 8–12 ottobre 1984, (Rome: Ed. Miscellanea Francescana, 1985), 492–503.

". . . *Extending a hand to all and leading all men to God through the Immaculata is a mission worth living, working, suffering, and even dying for*" (St. Maximilian Kolbe, SK 31).

Chapter Four

Consecration to the Immaculata in the Kolbean Spirit

St. Maximilian Kolbe rooted his Marian spirituality in the traditional principles of consecration (as we have seen in the third chapter.)

It is essential to the nature of consecration to the Immaculata in the *Militia Immaculatae* movement to become ever more fully the Immaculata's property under every aspect without limits and forever, and to be in her hands an instrument for the salvation of other souls (cf. SK 1329).

By his study in Mariology, his daily personal experiences, and his being attentive to the Spirit of God who was leading him, Fr. Kolbe, beloved son of the Virgin Mary, came to deepen and to enrich ever more profoundly his spirituality. He affirmed:

The Knights of the Immaculata [members of the *Militia Immaculatae* Movement] seek to become ever more truly the property of the Immaculata; to belong to her in an ever more perfect way and under every aspect without any exception. They wish to develop their understanding of what it means to belong to her so that they may enlighten, reinvigorate, and set on fire the souls living in their own environment, and make them similar to themselves. They desire to conquer these souls for the Immaculata, so that in their turn they may belong to her without reserve and may in this manner win an ever greater number of souls to her—may win the entire world, in fact, and do so in the shortest possible time.[1]

Consecration to Mary in Kolbe's spirit, as we already said, has its specific expression in the offering of oneself as a victim with apostolic intent.

Let us examine carefully the following letter, written on November 4, 1919:

> There are so many strayed and deceived souls enslaved by Satan, who are suffering and do not realize their ignorance and spiritual misery. Extending a hand to all and leading all men to God through the Immaculata, our Queen, is a mission worth living, working, suffering, and even dying for. (God willing, as martyrs).[2]

This expression *"To live, work, suffer, and even die for the Immaculata"* contains the essential aspects of the Church which are:

> Liturgy: prayer;
> Communion: charity;
> Ministry: service;
> Martyrdom: testimony.

The same expression reminds us of the four elements which form the true and genuine identity of a Christian:

consecrating one's life to Christ through Baptism;

living an authentic Christian life according to the Ten Commandments, the Beatitudes, and the teachings of the Church;

giving testimony by the sanctity of one's actions, a consequence and fruit of total love for God and neighbor;

evangelizing, *extending* one's hand to all, *suffering* with those who suffer, *dying each day to one's self*, and *sacrificing one's life* imitating the example of the Master.

In the light of St. Maximilian Kolbe's writings and life, we will try to illustrate this total consecration to the Immaculata.

We will seek to understand how to live and mirror it in our daily life as Catholics. We are aware that we will not grasp the entire richness of the Marian apostle.

However I believe that his intercession, Mary's mediation, and the power of the Holy Spirit will lead us to that height of sanctity which is proportionate to our attitudes of listening and responding generously.

Notes

[1] St. Maximilian Kolbe, Sketch, December 1937, *Gli Scritti di Massimiliano Kolbe, Eroe di Oświęcim e Beato della Chiesa*, translated by Immaculata Press from materials compiled and translated by Cristoforo Zambelli, 3 vols. (Florence: Cittá di Vita, 1976–78) 3:776.

[2] St. Maximilian Kolbe, Letter, November 4, 1919, *Gli Scritti di Massimiliano Kolbe*, 1:55.

Chapter Five

To Live in Mary: the Key to Sanctity

Vocation to Holiness

We know that in order to obtain eternal life it is necessary to die in the state of grace. But it is impossible to persevere in grace for a considerable length of time without struggling for progress, without striving for sanctity.

The Words of the divine Master are very clear:

"You must be perfect as your heavenly Father is perfect" (Mt 5:48).

"If anyone comes to me without turning his back on his father and mother, his wife and children, his brothers and sisters, indeed his very self, he cannot be my follower" (Lk 14:26).

"Enter through the narrow gate" (Mt 7:13).

St. Paul also repeats frequently to the faithful that they were chosen in order to become saints (cf. Eph 1:4).

St. Peter wants all his disciples to be saints as the One who called them to salvation (cf. 1 Pt 1:15).

In the Book of Revelation, St. John invites the virtuous to live on in their virtue and the holy ones in their holiness (cf. Rev 22:11).

All these exhortations and invitations bring forth within us the conviction that sanctity is the vocation of all Christians:

> All in the Church, whether they belong to the hierarchy or are cared for by it, are called to holiness, according to the apostle's saying: "For this is the will of God, your sanctification" (1 Th 4:3; cf. Eph 1:4). This holiness of the Church is constantly shown forth in the fruits of grace which the Spirit produces in the faithful and so it must be; it is expressed in many ways by the individuals who, each in his own state of life, tend to the perfection of love, thus sanctifying others; it appears in a certain way of its own in the practice of the counsels which have been usually called "evangelical."[1]

Then, the first duty of one who consecrates himself to the Immaculata in the *Militia Immaculatae* spirituality is to strive for sanctity. Fr. Kolbe says:

> It is only right that he who wants to dedicate himself to the sanctification of souls should begin with himself.[2]

Essence and Nature of Sanctity

There are many false notions of sanctity. Some perceive it as a call for an elite group, an emotional state, or an impractical utopia. Among the devout there are those who fool themselves as to the true nature of sanctity. St. Francis de Sales says that they paint a picture according to their own ideas and desires.[3] Some think to develop sanctity by the recitation of many prayers; others, in fasting and in austerity. Others confuse it with spiritual consolations, with fervor, believing they are perfect when they are flooded with the sentiment of joy, and others dedicate themselves only to exterior actions. Finally there are those who seek sanctity in ecstasies, in visions, or in extraordinary phenomena.

We affirm, instead, that the essence of sanctity is love.

"You shall love the Lord your God with your whole heart, with your whole soul, with all your mind. You shall love your neighbor as yourself" (Mt 22:37–39).

How can mankind (with its egoism, vices, and weaknesses) approach God and love Him above all? It is Mary's mission to draw man to Jesus Christ because she is the Mediatrix between human corruption and divine transcendence, because of the Incarnation of the Son of God.

St. Maximilian understood well this truth. Many times he affirmed:

We require God's grace in order to do good, and the soul can obtain that grace through prayer. At our disposal there is someone through

whom we can easily and surely obtain this: the
Mediatrix of all graces. All that is required is
that we really accept her and keep always closer
to her, that we love her always more ardently
in every temptation, difficulty, or trouble,
acknowledging her power, her universal mediation next to God, and that we turn to her with
total confidence. Then we too shall be capable
of everything (cf. Phil 4:13), but in Him who
gives us the strength through the Immaculata.[4]

Our struggle for sanctity does not have any limits.
Fr. Kolbe, in fact, teaches:

> The Cross, the manger, all the other mysteries
> in the life of Jesus are proof of his love for
> mankind. Who reflects upon it will repay that
> love with love. . . . Now, who loved the poor
> Jesus in the manger and on the Cross, more
> than his Blessed Mother? . . . Let us not limit
> our love; let us love Jesus with her Heart, for
> she loved Him with that very Heart. Let our
> love for God be the very love of the Immaculata.
> For this to be a reality we must be hers—entirely,
> completely, and in every way—hers.[5]

Following the teaching of the Gospel, one who
wishes to reach sanctity must begin by denying
one's very self. St. Maximilian asserts:

> One Saint said that when a house is afire, all
> within it is thrown out through the windows.
> So, too, the soul: when it is afire with the flame

of divine love, it casts out all that is unnecessary, and concentrates all in the divine love.[6]

Since no defect is too big and no sin is too great for God's merciful love, we can strive again for the highest sanctity if we trust in Mary and give ourselves totally to her.

Do not be surprised that within yourself you sense both good and evil. Whatever evil there is is from yourself, and all that is good flows through the hands of the Immaculate Mediatrix of grace from God. We must fight with our weaknesses without growing angry. We must place all our trust in her and through holy obedience she will bring us to heaven. Trust without limit in her and all your weaknesses will be turned about to your own good.[7]

Trust yourself in nothing; be careful, and confide in her without limit, at every moment or occasion of sin turn to her as a child to its mother and you will never fall. The saints affirm that anyone who prays to the Mother of God in time of temptation will most surely not sin, and who throughout life has recourse to her with confidence, will most surely be saved.[8]

It is neither difficult to love her nor is it impossible to follow her, for she asks of us only the perfect accomplishment of God's law:

Let us love her concretely, fulfilling all our duties as well as we can, from morning to night, since all this is the will of Jesus.[9]

Consecration to Mary infuses conviction, determination, and trust in one's soul.

A saint is not some old or senile fellow. . . . No, a saint must be quick-witted and enterprising and full of initiative. . . . He must be like an automobile, with all its accessories. The automobile is finely driven by the chauffeur, but it must run on its own power; the chauffeur gives speed, directs right and left, and turns. And, the automobile will be in best order when it is able to operate as the chauffeur wills: slow, when it is to go slow; fast, when it is to go fast; to the left, when it is to go to the left, and so on. Each of us must submit to this kind of direction, but ourselves must go forward, just like that automobile. Nobody has to push the car from the rear. If the Immaculata tells us to work here, why then, we must put all our energy into it, all our ardor, talent, and competence. If she orders us to rest, then we must rest. When it is time to recreate, then we must do that, too. Now, a soul that does everything in such a manner, already is doing very much good for the cause of the Immaculata.[10]

Our Duties

Our duties embrace the life-commitment that stems from Baptism and the long journey which leads us to fulfill our Christian life. We intend the exercise of Christian ascent which Jesus clearly expressed by the following words:

"If a man wishes to come after me, he must deny his very self, take up his cross, and begin to follow in my footsteps" (Mt 16:24).

Our duties also stress obedience to the Ten Commandments, which includes the practice of moral and Christian virtues and obedience to the Catholic Church and her Pastors. Finally, our duties emphasize one's obligations flowing from his state of life.

Catholics consecrated to Mary, then, serve God in joy in the different expressions of social, family, and religious life. They fulfill their mission in the plan of salvation whether in the priesthood, in consecrated life, or in married life.

By faith Catholics recognize God's will in the events of their daily lives. Even when the results do not measure up to their efforts, they remain serene. St. Maximilian bears witness to these affirmations and gives us encouragement and hope.

Let us not become attached to work, to our office, to dignities, to a place. Let everyone strive to do God's will—that is the summit of everything.[11]

The Immaculata looks at [one's] heart and will. . . . [When] someone, despite [his] best efforts, seems not to succeed, he should not worry, for the Immaculata is truly pleased with him, quite apart from the results.[12]

Fr. Kolbe was animated by the unshakable certitude that the degree of sanctity depends on our confidence in Mary and on our abandonment in her maternal Heart:

> Persons who have totally consecrated themselves to the Immaculata have already reached holiness, and the more they allow her to guide them in their spiritual life and apostolic activity, the more they participate in her holiness. [13]

> Have no doubt that her will is entirely united to God's will. It is a matter, then, of uniting our will to hers, and thus we will be united to God through her. [14]

> Rest confidently assured that he who belongs to her will not be lost, but the more he belongs to her, all the more so he belongs to Jesus and the Father. [15]

The possibility of our attaining sanctity does not depend on the environment, persons, and circumstances around us:

> Let everyone strive not so much to change his environment, as to perfect himself and personally to come closer to the Immaculata, and in this way all who draw near to her will reciprocally be drawn nearer to one another. [16]

He adds also:

> Ignore bad example. Remember that even among the Apostles there was Judas who abused the great grace of his vocation. Imitate the better ones. [17]

"Mary, having entered deeply into the history of salvation, . . . when she is the subject of preaching and worship . . . prompts the faithful to come to her Son, to his sacrifice and to the love of the Father" (LG 65).

Notes

[1] Vatican Council II, Dogmatic Constitution on the Church *Lumen Gentium* (1964), 39.

[2] St. Maximilian Kolbe, Conf., October 24, 1937, *Era Mariana*, translated by Immaculata Press from material compiled and translated by Fr. Luigi Faccenda, O.F.M. Conv. (Bologna: Edizioni dell'Immacolata, 1980), 42.

[3] Cf. St. Francis de Sales, *Introduction to the Devout Life*, first part of the Introduction.

[4] St. Maximilian Kolbe, Article published in *Rycerz Niepokalanej* ("Knight of the Immaculata" magazine) 10 (1937) (SK 1217), trans. in *Stronger than Hatred, A Collection of Spiritual Writings* (Brooklyn: New City Press, 1988), 108.

[5] St. Maximilian Kolbe, Address given September 4, 1937, *Maria Was His Middle Name: Day by Day with Blessed Maximilian Kolbe; Excerpts from His Writings and Addresses*, comp. Jerzy M. Domański, trans. Regis N. Barwig (Altadena, California: The Benzinger Sisters Publishers, 1977), 121.

[6] Ibid.

[7] St. Maximilian Kolbe, Letter to a Brother, *Maria Was His Middle Name*, 116.

[8] St. Maximilian Kolbe, *Rycerz Niepokalanej* 9 (1925) (SK 1100), *Maria Was His Middle Name*, 112.

[9] St. Maximilian Kolbe, Letter, October 14, 1937 (SK 751), *Stronger than Hatred*, 55.

[10] St. Maximilian Kolbe, Address given June 16, 1937, *Maria Was His Middle Name*, 98.

[11] St. Maximilian Kolbe, Address given June 9, 1937, *Maria Was His Middle Name*, 124.

[12] St. Maximilian Kolbe, Address given September 8, 1936, *Maria Was His Middle Name*, 125.

[13] St. Maximilian Kolbe, Letter, April 29, 1931 (SK 339), *Stronger than Hatred*, 114.

[14] St. Maximilian Kolbe, Letter, April 18, 1934 (SK 579), *Maria Was His Middle Name*, 96.

[15] St. Maximilian Kolbe, Letter, October 10, 1935, *Gli Scritti di Massimiliano Kolbe, Eroe di Oświecim e Beato della Chiesa*, translated by Immaculata Press from material compiled and translated by Cristoforo Zambelli, 3 vols. (Florence: Città di Vita, 1976–78), 2:201–8.

[16] St. Maximilian Kolbe, Letter, December 3, 1940, *Gli Scritti di Massimiliano Kolbe*, 2:567.

[17] St. Maximilian Kolbe, Letter, January 3, 1927, *Gli Scritti di Massimiliano Kolbe*, 1:264.

Chapter Six

The Consecration Lived by St. Maximilian Kolbe

In order to deepen our understanding of total consecration to the Immaculata, let us reflect on Fr. Kolbe's example.

St. Maximilian's imitation of and consecration to Mary may be considered in the light of Pope Paul VI's Apostolic Exhortation *Marialis Cultus*. In this precious document the Holy Father offered the Blessed Virgin as the model of the Church in divine worship. He outlined the four attitudes of Mary, presenting her as the *Attentive Virgin*, the *Virgin in Prayer*, the *Virgin Mother* and, finally, the *Virgin Presenting Offerings*.

Of course, Fr. Kolbe was not aware of this document, but we know how deep his understanding of Mary's mystery was! He knew intimately the Immaculate Conception and her relationships with God and mankind. Then, we can find these four attitudes of Mary reflected in his life.

Mary was the Attentive Virgin (cf. MC 17). She placed herself in an attitude of listening to divine inspirations, to Sacred Scripture, to her guides, and to Jesus Himself. Following her example Fr. Kolbe placed himself in an attitude of listening to God's will in his life. He heeded the voice and example of his family. He listened to interior inspirations, from the first vision of the two crowns—the white and red ones—to the generous offering of his life in the concentration camp of Auschwitz. He heard God's call; and when he understood his place in the plan of salvation, he did not hesitate to follow it and became a Franciscan priest. In particular, he was attentive when he perceived the unique role of Mary in man's redemption and consequently founded the *Militia Immaculatae*.

Mary—Pope Paul VI teaches—is also the Virgin in Prayer.

> She appears as such in the visit to the mother of the Precursor, when she pours out her soul in expressions glorifying God, and expressions of humility, faith, and hope. This prayer is the Magnificat. . . . At Cana, Mary appears once more as the Virgin in Prayer: when she tactfully told her Son of a temporal need, she also obtained an effect of grace, namely, that Jesus, in working the first of his "signs," confirmed his disciples' faith in Him (cf. Jn 2:1–12). Likewise, the last description of Mary's life presents her as praying. The Apostles "joined in continuous prayer, together with several women, including Mary the Mother of Jesus, and with his brothers" (Acts 1:14). We have here the prayerful presence

of Mary in the early Church and in the Church throughout all ages, for having been assumed into heaven she has not abandoned her mission of intercession and salvation.[1]

Fr. Kolbe, following in her footsteps, was a man of prayer. He lived the deepest interior life. During the day, many times he invoked Mary and implored her: "Immaculata, tell me who you are, what you want of me! Tell me how I can draw my brothers and sisters to you!" In jail and in the concentration camp he prayed the rosary and spoke about the divine mysteries with his companions. Even in the starvation bunker where he died he prayed until the last moment: "Ave Maria! Ave Maria!" One of his numerous teachings about prayer follows:

Living a life of prayer

Indeed, prayer is the most efficacious means of giving peace to souls, filling them with happiness and bringing them closer to God's love. Prayer renews the world. Prayer is the indispensable condition for the rebirth and life of each person. Through prayer, St. Thérèse having never left her cloister, became the patroness of all the missions and not only in a nominal sense, as experience proves. Let us pray, pray well and much, vocally and mentally, and we will experience how the Immaculata will more and more possess our souls and how in every way we will become more like her.

We will see how our faults will disappear,

how our bad habits weaken, and how mildly yet powerfully we will be able to go forward in our union with God. Exterior activity is good, but it is necessarily of secondary importance, and even less, in comparison with the interior life, the life of silence, prayer, and love for God. . . . To the extent that we will burn with the love of God, to that extent will we inflame it in the hearts of others.[2]

Fr. Kolbe was also like a loving mother to his men and to all his brothers and sisters. He always gave special attention to the young aspirants at Niepokalanów (the "City of the Immaculata," which he founded in Poland) and to the sick. He comforted his fellow captives and shared his bread with them. He held the hands of the dying and closed their eyes as they passed from this world to their eternal reward. Being totally Mary's, he modeled his heart on hers (cf. MC 19), and he nourished within himself a universal love for all mankind and for each person in particular.

He, like Mary the Virgin Presenting Offerings (cf. MC 20), suffered and presented offerings. When his physical suffering limited his strength and apostolic activity, when he was given the cruelest labors in the concentration camp—only because he was a priest and a Pole, or they found him with a rosary in his hands—he did not complain but was able to offer up everything out of love. He was a man consumed by a love without reserve:

"There is no greater love than this: to lay down one's life for one's friends" (Jn 15:13).

The key of his heroism was his total consecration to the Immaculata.

Contemplation and intimate union with Mary, the Virgin in Prayer, the Attentive Virgin, the Virgin Mother, and the Virgin Presenting Offerings should lead us, as Fr. Kolbe, to give testimony to the Gospel message in our lives.

Thus in the Kolbean style of total consecration to the Immaculata, Catholics may live the fullness of their baptismal vows.

Notes

[1] Pope Paul VI, Apostolic Exhortation for the Right Ordering and Development of Devotion to the Blessed Virgin Mary *Marialis Cultus* (February 2, 1974), 18.

[2] St. Maximilian Kolbe, Letter, September 10, 1940, *Gli Scritti di Massimiliano Kolbe, Eroe di Oświęcim e Beato della Chiesa*, translated by Immaculata Press from material compiled and translated by Cristoforo Zambelli, 3 vols. (Florence: Città di Vita, 1976–78), 2:538.

Chapter Seven

The Four Pillars
of Total Consecration

I would like to share with you some reflections on four realities which I call "the four pillars of total consecration to the Immaculata in Kolbean spirituality": *interior life, obedience, heroic charity, and suffering out of love.*

Interior Life: Union Between
Contemplation and Action

Jesus said "I am the vine, you are the branches" (Jn 15:5). In this wonderful and mysterious statement we discover the vital relationship between man and God which does not consist merely in the passage of sap from the vine into the branch, but requires an intense union and communication in order that the fruit might be abundant and lasting.

"He who lives in me and I in him, will produce abundantly, for apart from me you can do nothing" (Jn 15:5).

Hence the necessity of an ever deeper interior life which constitutes the true essence of sanctity; thus the soul is able to encounter God fully in every instant of life, in every expression of activity or apostolate, and in any stage of life's journey.

In this way it is possible to realize a true harmony between action and contemplation which confers a contemplative force to action and an intention essentially active to contemplation. In fact, if action is seen as the necessary fruit of contemplation and contemplation as the continual nourishment of action, there is no peril that action would impoverish the spiritual life or contemplation would restrain itself in an abstract vision of Christian life.

I think this was Fr. Kolbe's style in living the union between action and contemplation. I also see a similarity in St. Paul's teachings:

> "I am certain that neither death nor life, neither angels nor principalities, neither the present nor the future . . . nor any other creature, will be able to separate us from the love of God that comes to us in Christ Jesus, Our Lord" (Rom 8:38–39).

In imitation of the Virgin in Prayer, each Christian should strive to nurture his interior life with a truly prayerful and sacramental life, including meditation, silence and recollection, and even pauses from his daily activity. Above all he should strive to live and work with great purity of intention which permits him to see God in every action from the most sublime to the most menial. In such a way all things are directed to Him with love and accepted as a sign of his immense love.

Since the total offering to the Immaculata means "to belong to her as her own property" (cf. SK 1334), obedience becomes the virtue most recommended by St. Maximilian.

Obedience, in fact, means total conformity to the salvific will of God and consists in allowing the Immaculata to guide our lives freely. "How to recognize her will? The only certain way is by obedience to God's representatives."[1]

"He who listens to you, listens to me" (Lk 10:16).

Thus, important means by which we may live this spirit of obedience are the attentive and docile listening to the Word of God, the Holy Father and the Church's Magisterium, and also the events, situations, and obligations of our daily life.

Such is the full essence of holiness: accord with God's will. The soul which has determined that its will be one with God's senses an unspeakable happiness; it possesses peace and serenity, and that immovable foundation which is God Himself.[2]

The fulfillment of God's will is love, and love is the very heart of holiness. Not in mortification, nor in prayer, nor in work, nor in rest, but only in obedience do we find the merit and the essential quality of holiness.[3]

In the Gospel we contemplate Our Lady as the Attentive Virgin, who made her life a continual yes to God's will. In his Marian Encyclical, Pope John Paul II wrote:

At the Annunciation Mary entrusted herself to God completely, with full submission of intellect and will, manifesting the *"obedience of faith"* to Him who spoke to her through his messenger.[4]

Fr. Kolbe echoes the same teaching:

Let us pray much that we would understand more and more what the Immaculata said at the Annunciation: "Behold the handmaid of the Lord, be it done unto me according to your word." As God wills, so be it. In this thought all happiness is contained, already here on earth, all destiny fulfilled. God created us . . . [to] be his instruments, that is why He draws us to love Himself, and rewards us or punishes us.

Desirous that souls become perfect and like unto Him, He showers them with graces. But souls must cooperate with divine grace, and permit themselves to be led. Let us beg our Blessed Mother that she might teach us how our soul might be a "handservant" of the Lord, as was her own. God did not reveal Himself directly to the Mother of God, but rather through a messenger. We too have divine messengers. . . . Let us pray that we would know how to say to every one of these messengers: God's will be done. And in this is everything that we are placed upon this earth to learn and it is our task to teach this to the whole world, so that the will of every human being might be in accord with God's will—through the Immaculata.[5]

Heroic Charity: Readiness to Give One's Life for One's Brethren

This is the heart of the Gospel which calls us to love our neighbors as Jesus did:

"This is my commandment: love one another as I have loved you" (Jn 15:12).

"I give you a new commandment: love one another. Such as my love has been for you, so must your love be for each other. This is how all will know you for my disciples: by your love for one another" (Jn 13:34–35).

Heroic charity also characterized the whole earthly life of the Virgin Mother, as we can see in the Gospels: from the Visitation, to her solicitous presence at the wedding feast of Cana, to the Cenacle. She, who at the Annunciation called herself the "handmaid of the Lord," became the first of those who, by serving Christ in others, with humility and patience, lead their brothers and sisters to salvation. Now, in heaven, the glory of serving does not cease to be her royal exaltation as she continues to care for all of us (cf. LG 62 and RM 41).

She showed the highest expression of her maternal love at the foot of the Cross

> . . . where she stood, in keeping with the divine plan, enduring with her only begotten Son the intensity of his suffering, associated herself with his sacrifice in her mother's heart, and lovingly consenting to the immolation of the victim which was born of her. Finally, she was given by the same Christ Jesus dying on the Cross as a Mother to his disciple, with these words: "Woman, behold your son" (Jn 19:26–27).[6]

Through our consecration to her we are called to share in her unlimited charity. This attitude of self-giving, however, such as the supreme offering of Fr. Kolbe in the concentration camp, implies a daily effort. It requires a continual giving of ourselves so as to become instruments of love and communion. This attitude must be the focus of our relationships with friends, relatives, and all our brothers and sisters, with the Church by obedience to her teachings, within the Church, and with all mankind, without distinction of race and culture.

In order to realize a genuine mutual love, we need to live in an attitude of interior poverty and humility; we must always be ready to extend our hand to others and to forgive one another.

> The essence of mutual love does not consist in the fact that no one causes us grief, which is impossible in living together with other people,

but that we learn to forgive one another immediately and always more perfectly. Then we shall have great confidence in reciting the invocation contained in the Lord's Prayer: "and forgive us our trespasses as we forgive those who trespass against us" (Mt 6:12). If we had nothing or very little to forgive others, we would be in great trouble, indeed.

Let us use every opportunity to exercise patience, humility. . . . Let us prove through our actions that with the Immaculata's help we can do everything, since that is what we proclaim. Let us put in her our confidence, let us pray and go ahead in life with peace and serenity.[7]

Supreme Offering: Suffering Willed Out of Love

The life of man consists of three parts: preparation for work, work itself, and suffering. Through these stages God brings us closer to Himself. The more a soul is striving for sanctity, the sooner it is readied for the third stage placing its love for the Immaculata on the foundation of suffering out of love.[8]

Suffering willed out of love—the fourth pillar of our consecration—means to accept and love sorrows and sufferings in our life, and to make a total offering of ourselves to God for the redemption of the world through Mary.

Those who consecrate themselves to the Immaculata, the Virgin Presenting Offerings, should not ask for any special suffering, like sickness, trials, or martyrdom. Instead, they, serenely, should leave her the total freedom to use themselves as instruments and to do whatever she wants. They place themselves in the attitude of embracing everything with a humble spirit of faith and love in union with Christ Crucified. Christian life, in fact, consists in participating in Christ's life. Christian perfection is the perfect imitation of Him who made of his life a total self-offering. St. Paul writes:

"Be imitators of God as his dear children. Follow the way of love, even as Christ loved you. He gave Himself for us as an offering to God, a gift of pleasing fragrance" (Eph 5:1–2).

What suffering did Christ choose? What suffering did Mary choose? What suffering did Fr. Kolbe choose? They did not pick or choose one or the other. They lived in a spirit of total abandonment and immolation, in complete fulfillment of the Father's will. "Behold I come to do your will O my God" (cf. Heb 10:7); "Behold the handmaid of the Lord" (Lk 1:38). Therefore, when we speak of suffering willed out of love, we are not singling out physical suffering. One cannot say he has arrived because he has continual headaches or because he has a tumor or other physical ailment.

There is another form of suffering, no less heavy than the physical. This is the moral or psychological suffering. It does not attack the muscles or cells but the most intimate part of ourselves. It manifests itself in depressions, breakdowns, misunderstandings, betrayals. They are extremely painful. But not even this encompasses totally this fourth column.

There is another aspect of suffering which Christ during his Passion, Mary at the foot of the Cross, St. Thérèse of Lisieux, Fr. Kolbe, and many souls experienced. We call this the dark night of the soul, the desert of the spirit, the tunnel of death in which one feels completely abandoned by everyone and, above all, by God.

Fr. Kolbe lived this total immolation in all the stages of his life, growing ever more in his love for man, the Immaculata, and God to the point of giving his life for another man.

From the examples of Jesus, Mary, and Fr. Kolbe we learn that suffering lived out of love, little by little, enables us to become more attentive to others' needs and to share in their sufferings.

Christ, God become man, made Himself subject to suffering in order fully to understand our suffering. Mary at the foot of the Cross was pierced with sorrow and there became the mother of all mankind. All of this bears witness to the fact that only in suffering can we truly become united brethren. After love, suffering is the most universal and cohesive force.

Suffering out of love: "I find my joy in the suffering I endure for you. In my own flesh I fill up what is lacking in the sufferings of Christ for the sake of his body, the Church" (Col 1:24), so that each person may know Our Lord, who saved man by his suffering.

Let us conclude with the following thoughts from Fr. Kolbe which may lead us to perceive, in the light of the Spirit, the true meaning of this fourth pillar:

God in his infinite goodness desires to draw us to Himself, to encourage us to work already here on earth, so that we might have something of a foretaste of eternal happiness, whose fullness will be our crown. Striving with all our strength to correspond to the invitations of God's grace and increase his glory through the Immaculate Virgin in ourselves and in others, we sometimes experience the happy peace of a child who, having placed himself unreservedly into the hands of his mother, worries about nothing, fears nothing, ever trusting in the wisdom, goodness, and strength of his mother. Sometimes it will happen that the tempest will be all-encompassing, lightning will strike, and thunder will roar, but we who are totally in the hands of the Immaculata can be certain that nothing will harm us, as long as our heavenly Mother is with us and as long as she does not will it. [9]

No temptation is a sin. No matter how long the temptation might last, it is not a sin, but much depends on how the soul reacts before it becomes a field of merit. As to the method of the battle, do not begin to doubt or fall into nervousness, but peacefully have recourse to the Immaculata and make nothing of it all, and simply do not have the time for it. Keep busy with something else. Sometimes people worry or fret. There is no need for it, for Satan uses this to tire a soul. I repeat, therefore, no temptation in itself does any harm to a soul, as long as, on our part, there is no consent.[10]

Sometimes our health and our own duties do not allow us to suffer the hardships of penance, even though everybody admits that the road of our earthly existence is covered with small crosses. The acceptance of these crosses in the spirit of penance is the vast field where we can exercise penance. Besides, we are to fulfill our everyday duties and the will of God in every instant of our lives. The latter, which we must do perfectly in every action, word, or thought, demands giving up a lot of things we like: and this is a plentiful source of penance.

However, Jesus urges us not to be sad when doing penance, but to do it for love.

A soul that loves God is always ready to please, with every thought, word, and action, throughout one's entire existence. And should any affection be sacrificed in order to give joy to God, we should consider ourselves fortunate to have the opportunity to prove our unselfish love.

That is why the saints were always willing to

make sacrifices and to suffer. In fact, that was how they could prove the purity of their love; in the cross their love was purified and every affection that was contrary to it was rooted out.

Thus, we can all do penance, without considering our health conditions, the type of occupations and duties that our own status or calling in life calls for; in fact, we can do penance every moment of our lives, as long as we do it for love.[11]

Love lives on, nourishes itself on sacrifice. Let us thank the Immaculata for interior peace, for the ecstasy of love. Still, we should remember that even though these things are good and beautiful, they are absolutely not the essence of love, and that love, in fact, perfect love, can exist even without them.

The peak of love is the state in which Jesus happened to find Himself on the Cross when He cried: "My God, my God, why have you forsaken me?" (Mt 27:46).

There is no love without sacrifice. And this includes sacrificing our senses, especially our eyes . . . , our taste, our hearing, and . . . above all, sacrificing our reason and our will in holy obedience.[12]

Notes

[1] St. Maximilian Kolbe, Autograph manuscript on the *Militia Immaculatae*, *Maria Was His Middle Name: Day by Day with Blessed Maximilian Kolbe; Excerpts from His Writings and Addresses*, comp. Jerzy M. Domański, trans. Regis N. Barwig (Altadena, California: The Benzinger Sisters Publishers, 1977), 96.

[2] St. Maximilian Kolbe, Address given April 2, 1938, *Maria Was His Middle Name*, 78.

[3] St. Maximilian Kolbe, Address given June 23, 1936, *Maria Was His Middle Name*, 78.

[4] Pope John Paul II, Encyclical Letter on the Blessed Virgin Mary in the Life of the Pilgrim Church *Redemptoris Mater* (March 25, 1987), 13.

[5] St. Maximilian Kolbe, Address given April 2, 1938, *Maria Was His Middle Name*, 79.

[6] Vatican Council II, Dogmatic Constitution on the Church *Lumen Gentium* (1964), 58.

[7] St. Maximilian Kolbe, Letter, January 9, 1941, *Gli Scritti di Massimiliano Kolbe, Eroe di Oświęcim e Beato della Chiesa*, translated by Immaculata Press from material compiled and translated by Cristoforo Zambelli, 3 vols. (Florence: Città di Vita, 1976–78), 2:577.

[8] St. Maximilian Kolbe, Address given August 28, 1939, *Maria Was His Middle Name*, 174.

[9] St. Maximilian Kolbe, Autograph manuscript on the *Militia Immaculatae*, *Maria Was His Middle Name*, 131.

[10] St. Maximilian Kolbe, Address given August 16, 1936, *Maria Was His Middle Name*, 110.

[11] St. Maximilian Kolbe, Unpublished Article (1940) (SK 1303), *Stronger than Hatred, a Collection of Spiritual Writings* (Brooklyn: New City Press, 1988), 100–101.

[12] St. Maximilian Kolbe, Letter, April 9, 1933 (SK 503), *Stronger than Hatred*, 101.

Chapter Eight

Missionary Dynamism of Consecration to the Immaculata

The Church on earth is *by its very nature missionary.*[1]

As members of the living Christ, incorporated into Him and made like Him by Baptism, Confirmation, and the Eucharist, all the faithful have an obligation to collaborate in the expansion and spread of his Body, so that they might bring it to fullness as soon as possible (Cf. Eph 4:13).[2]

In order to accomplish his plan of salvation as soon as possible, God willed to need us. He wanted to give us a place in this plan: He made us his collaborators. In every age he called many people to be priests, missionaries, consecrated persons so that by their example, word, and above all the offering of their whole lives, his redemptive work might be brought to all people and nations.

The call of the Lord is also addressed to every person who lives in this world, as the Holy Father John Paul II wrote in the Apostolic Exhortation

In 1930 Fr. Kolbe set out for Japan. There he founded Mugenzai-No-Sono, "Garden of the Immaculata", a Marian missionary center.

Christifideles Laici on the lay faithful. He repeated the words of the Gospel: "You too go into my vineyard" (Mt 20:4).

The call is a concern not only of pastors, clergy, and men and women religious. *The call is addressed to everyone*: *lay people* as well *are personally called* by the Lord from whom they receive a mission on behalf of the Church and the world.[3]

Consecration to Mary draws us in a deeper way into this mission of the Church. Therefore, it is not just for our personal sanctification, but it becomes a calling to work for the sanctification of others.

Mission of the Church

After the care of all mankind under the Cross was entrusted to Mary, Jesus cried out, "*I thirst*." This cry of Christ, his thirst for souls, reverberated in Mary's heart, and she continues to communicate it to all her children. This is the dynamic dimension of consecration which St. Maximilian perceived and developed and which unites the *Militia Immaculatae* movement to the very mission of the Church.

Therefore, consecration to the Immaculata in the Kolbean spirituality is clearly a total offering of ourselves "with apostolic intent." The true experience of consecration leads us to radiate the presence of Mary around us.

The Immaculata is our ideal. We must radiate [Mary] in the midst of our surroundings, winning souls for her, so that souls might open to her, that she might rule within them all, everywhere in the world, without regard to various races, nationalities, languages, as well as in the hearts of all who will be on earth until the end of time—such is our ideal. And that her life would be deepened in us day to day, hour upon hour, moment after moment, and that without limit—such is our ideal. And that her life would similarly unfold in each and every soul, that is or will ever be—such is our ideal.[4]

Those who consecrate themselves to Mary and experience her strength in temptations and her consolation in difficulties feel the desire to share their joy with others so that they too may be drawn to Mary. In this way Mary will enlighten their hearts, warm them with her maternal love, and enkindle them with the fire of charity which burns in the divine Heart of Jesus.

The Immaculata comes down on earth as a good Mother in the midst of her children to help them to save their souls. She desires the conversion and sanctification of all souls, without exception. She makes use of human instruments to attain this end, as we note in her apparitions. But such are extraordinary happenings. More frequently she inspired her loving children to cooperate with her in ordinary circumstances of daily life. These souls consecrated to her live by her and frequently think about her. They love her wholeheartedly and endeavor to know her desires, whether from her own lips or those entrusted by her in the form of interior aspirations. They strive to make her will known and loved, drawing more and more souls to a more perfect knowledge of her and a more heartfelt love of Jesus' divine Heart in and through her.

Thousands of such souls the Immaculata inspires in every period of history. A good number, too, have organized themselves into groups, so that in a common effort they might still better serve their Blessed Lady. One of the youngest of these groups striving to the attainment of that purpose, namely, the winning of souls for the Immaculate Virgin, and through her for the Most Sacred Heart of Jesus, is the *Militia of the Immaculata*.[5]

Where is our apostolic field? Fr. Kolbe answers:

Let everyone regard his surroundings, relatives, acquaintances, working companions, place of residence as the territory of his mission to win all for the Immaculata; to this end let every influence and capacity be employed.[6]

Through our consecration Mary not only calls us to share deeply in her mission of giving Christ to the world, but she realizes it through us.

What means are we to use to collaborate with her?

The ordinary means that promote the good of souls, namely, good example, prayer, work and patience in suffering. By good example we draw our brother closer to us; by prayer, by sacrifice, by patience, the grace of divine guidance; by external works the task is perfected, unless, of course the souls, which we desire to win for Mary should knowingly and willingly resist the influx of divine grace. Therefore, the *Militia Immaculatae* employs every means that is lawful and just and that leads to the desired end.[7]

The Church confirms:

For their work, prayers and apostolic endeavors, their ordinary married and family life, their daily labor, their mental and physical relaxation, if carried out in the Spirit, and even the hardships of life if patiently borne—all of these become spiritual sacrifices acceptable to God through Jesus Christ (cf. 1 Pt 2:5). During the celebration of the Eucharist these sacrifices are most lovingly offered to the Father along with the Lord's Body. Thus as worshipers whose every deed is holy, the lay faithful consecrate the world itself to God, [and become a help for its conversion and belief in the Gospel].[8]

The presence of Mary within us fills us with a universal love. She shares with us her own concern for the salvation and sanctification of all souls.

We must always develop more fervently and intensely the action of conquering all souls for the Immaculata. . . . We must always remember that Poland and Japan are not the only nations that exist under the sun. An immense number of hearts beat beyond these boundaries. And so when will the Knights of the Immaculata go among them? . . . When will they lead all the hearts of men to the Most Sacred Heart of Jesus by the white ladder of the Immaculata, that which our holy father Francis saw? . . . Care must be taken to nourish souls with the Immaculata so that they will assimilate and live the life of the Immaculata. Every thought, action and suffering of the Immaculata was a most perfect act of love toward God, toward Jesus. We must, therefore, say this to all the souls and to each one of them in particular, to those who live today on earth and to those who will live. Say it with example, with the living word, the printed word, through the radio, painting, sculpture, etc. Say what and how the Immaculata in concrete circumstances of actual life and in every state had thought, spoken, and done to ignite on earth the most perfect love of her Heart toward the divine Heart. [9]

Fr. Kolbe challenges us:

Considering all that I have said above—with my hand on my heart—can I say that I did all that was in my power to do, so that I neglected nothing and that I did everything in the best possible way? Oh, no! Therefore, I thank you very much for [your] prayers and I ask for more prayers so that sweetly and strongly I may serve the Immaculata: that all and each one in particular may surpass me a thousand times; and I, that I may surpass them in turn yet a million times; and that they may then surpass me a billion times in a noble race. It is not a question that I, this or that one does more, but that the most be done for the Immaculata. She must take possession of every soul as soon as possible in the most perfect way, to live and act in each soul, to love the divine Heart, the divine Love, God, in each soul.[10]

What is the ultimate goal of all this apostolic dynamism?

It is a matter of deepening more fervently the love of the creature toward the Creator.[11]

If we work all together in the vineyard of the Lord, we are sure that the whole world will be transformed and that God will revive the hearts of mankind, triumphing over error and sin in view of the definitive coming of his kingdom. For this reason, I challenge you to offer everything you have for the salvation of mankind: your time, love, and your life. Do this with the Immaculata! Do this in the footsteps of St. Maximilian! Do this at this special moment of the Church!

Notes

[1] Vatican Council II, Decree on the Missionary Activity of the Church *Ad Gentes* (1965), 2.

[2] Ibid., 36

[3] Pope John Paul II, Post-Synodal Apostolic Exhortation on the Vocation and the Mission of the Lay Faithful in the Church and in the World *Christifideles Laici* (December 30, 1988), 2.

[4] St. Maximilian Kolbe, Article published in *Rycerz Niepokalanej* ("Knight of the Immaculata" magazine) 8 (1936) (SK 1210), trans. in *Maria Was His Middle Name: Day by Day with Blessed Maximilian Kolbe; Excerpts from His Writings and Addresses*, comp. Jerzy M. Domański, trans. Regis N. Barwig (Altadena, California: The Benziger Sisters Publishers, 1977), 145–46.

[5] St. Maximilian Kolbe, Sketch, May 2–15, 1939 (SK 1323), *Maria Was His Middle Name*, 144.

[6] St. Maximilian Kolbe, *Rycerz Niepokalanej* 7 (1926) (SK 1127), *Maria Was His Middle Name*, 154.

[7] St. Maximilian Kolbe, Pamphlet on the *Militia Immaculatae* (March 1938) (SK 1226), *Maria Was His Middle Name*, 152–53.

[8] Vatican Council II, Dogmatic Constitution on the Church *Lumen Gentium* (1964), 34.

[9] St. Maximilian Kolbe, Letter, October 30, 1935 (SK 647), *St. Maximilian Kolbe Apostle of Our Difficult Age*, trans. Antonio Ricciardi, O.F.M. Conv. (Boston: St. Paul Editions, 1982), 199–200.

[10] Ibid.

[11] Ibid.

Chapter Nine

Practical Preparation for Consecration to the Immaculata

Consecration to the Immaculata is a totally free act, accepted and lived as a gift. Its essence is the total offering of ourselves to Mary.

In order to prepare ourselves seriously to make the act of consecration to the Immaculata, we should deepen our knowledge of Church doctrine about Our Lady and the meaning of our consecration to her. (See the preceding chapters and any other current material.)

On the fixed date during Mass, if it is possible, the person recites the formula of his consecration which should be renewed frequently. As a sign of his consecration he will wear the Miraculous Medal and above all will live as a true child and apostle of Mary.

The act of consecration may be made publicly, in the presence of a priest, or personally, in a simple way.

All baptized Christians (children, young people, adults, the elderly, families, religious and priests) may consecrate themselves to the Immaculata. Even those who belong to groups, associations, religious communities (parochial or diocesan), are invited to consecrate themselves to Mary. In fact, this consecration will not conflict with, but rather enrich one's vocation and apostolic activity with the constant and maternal presence of the Immaculata.

Even those who have strayed from the Faith and those who are not in full communion with the Church may consecrate themselves to Mary, for she will help them to change and to begin a new life which may lead them even to the highest sanctity.

St. Maximilian said:

Here we have the ladder, the platform, the pedestal from which we might reach up to the Most Sacred Heart of Jesus. If anyone falls into sin, falls deeply into bad habits, despises God and his grace, ignores good example, pays no attention to the inspirations that can save, and becomes unworthy of further graces, should he despair? Never, absolutely never! For from God he has a Mother who with a warm heart follows his every action, word, and thought. She does not look upon whether he is worthy of the grace of loving kindness and mercy. She is only a Mother of mercy, and hastens, even when not invoked, there where she finds the greatest misery in souls. . . . She needs only enter into a heart, though it still be filled with misery, sullied by sin and vice, and she cannot let it be lost, but begs God for the soul to be enlightened, to follow the light of grace and of reason and to take on strength of will, that it might come to its senses and rise again.[1]

Whoever makes the consecration is not required to practice any particular exercises of piety. However, it is suggested to incorporate the following practices which belong to the rich tradition of the Church:

daily recitation of three Hail Marys, followed by the ejaculatory prayer: "O Mary, conceived without sin, pray for us who have recourse to you, and for those who do not have recourse to you, especially for the enemies of the Holy Church and for those recommended to you."

practice of the First Saturdays, as Our Lady requested at Fatima.

daily renewal of the act of consecration, at least by reciting a short formula prayer.

frequent recitation of the Rosary according to the teachings of the Apostolic Exhortation *Marialis Cultus*, 42.

daily meditation based on Sacred Scripture or on a formative book. This is a basis and a secret for growing in sanctity. A daily personal encounter with God is also suggested (10–15 minutes).

fervent attendance at Mass and frequent reception of Holy Communion and the Sacrament of Reconciliation.

Catholics are encouraged to join a movement approved by the Church in which they may share with others this Marian way of life. One such movement is the *Militia Immaculatae* founded by St. Maximilian Kolbe. Any Catholic who would like to belong to this ecclesial association may ask to be enrolled in an official canonical center of the *Militia Immaculatae*.

As Fr. Kolbe many times suggested, it would be good to receive the Sacrament of Reconciliation before making the consecration, in order to acquire the plenary indulgence which the Church grants on the enrollment in the *Militia Immaculatae* movement.

Notes

[1] St. Maximilian Kolbe, Article published in *Rycerz Niepokalanej* ("Knight of the Immaculata" magazine) 6 (1925) (SK 1094), trans. in *Maria Was His Middle Name: Day by Day with Blessed Maximilian Kolbe; Excerpts from His Writings and Addresses*, comp. Jerzy M. Domański, trans. Regis N. Barwig (Altadena, California: The Benzinger Sisters Publishers, 1977), 50.

Chapter Ten

Rite of Consecration to the Immaculata

The following is a suggested simple rite for personal, family, or community consecration to Mary.

Opening Prayer (suggested)

All: I adore you, our heavenly Father, because you have placed in the most pure womb of Mary your only-begotten Son.

I adore you, O Son of God, because you deigned to enter the womb of Mary and become her true, real Son.

I adore you, O Holy Spirit, because you deigned to form in her immaculate womb the body of the Son of God.

I adore you, O most holy Trinity, O one God in three persons, for having ennobled the Immaculata in a manner so divine. (St. Maximilian Kolbe)

Leader: *Reading from the Holy Gospel according to John*

Near the cross of Jesus there stood his mother, his mother's sister, Mary the wife of Clopas, and Mary Magdalene. Seeing his mother there with the disciple whom he loved, Jesus said to his mother, "Woman, there is your son." In turn he said to the disciple, "There is your mother." From that hour onward, the disciple took her into his care (Jn 19:25–27).

Leader: Dear . . . , the Lord has inspired you to entrust yourself wholly to Mary in order to become an instrument of his grace for the conversion and sanctification of all mankind. Do you wish, therefore, with the help of the Holy Spirit, to live your life in perfect union with the Immaculata and to be for all your brothers and sisters a light and an example of Christian life?

All: Yes, I do.

Leader: Let us invoke the Holy Spirit praying together:

All: Come, Holy Spirit, Creator, come
From your bright heavenly throne;

Come, take possession of our souls,
And make them all your own.

You are called the Paraclete,
Best gift of God above;
The living spring, the living fire,
Sweet unction and true love.

You who are sevenfold in your grace,
Finger of God's right hand,
His promise, teaching little ones
To speak and understand.

Oh guide our minds with your blest light,
With love our hearts inflame
And with strength, which never decays
Confirm our mortal frame.

Far from us drive our hellish foe,
True peace unto us bring;
And through all perils lead us safe
Beneath your sacred wing.

Through you may we the Father know,
Through you the eternal Son,
And you the Spirit of them both
Thrice-blessed three in one.

All glory to the Father be,
And to his risen Son,
The like to you, great Paraclete,
While endless ages run. Amen.

Renewal of Baptismal Promises

Leader: The act of total consecration to Our Lady will lead you to live fully your Baptism. For this reason we now renew the promises that our parents and godparents made for us.

Do you reject sin, so as to live in the freedom of God's children?

All: I do.

Leader: Do you reject the glamour of evil, and refuse to be mastered by sin?

All: I do.

Leader: Do you reject Satan, father and prince of darkness?

All: I do.

Leader: Do you believe in God, the Father almighty, creator of heaven and earth?

All: I do.

Leader: Do you believe in Jesus Christ, his only Son, Our Lord, who was born of the Virgin Mary, was crucified, died, and was buried, rose from the dead, and is now seated at the right hand of the Father?

All: I do.

Leader: Do you believe in the Holy Spirit, the
           Holy Catholic Church, the communion of
           saints, the forgiveness of sins, the resur-
           rection of the body, and life everlasting?

All: I do.

Consecration to the Immaculata

*(Each person is invited to make and live out the act
of consecration. The formula prayer is to be chosen
according to one's age or state of life. See pp. 104–
114.)*

Blessing and Imposition of the Miraculous Medal

Leader: This medal is a sign of our total consecra-
           tion to Mary and a sign of her maternal
           protection in this life.

           *If a priest leads the rite, he may bless the medal with
           the following prayer:*

Priest: Our help is in the name of the Lord.

All: Who made heaven and earth.

Priest: Let us pray.

           Almighty and merciful God, who through
           the many apparitions of the Immaculate
           Virgin on earth has deigned to work great

wonders, bless + this medal, so that all who wear it in love and veneration might enjoy your protection and gain your mercy. Through Christ Our Lord.

All: Amen.

The medal is given to each person, while the leader says each time or once for all:

Leader: Receive this holy medal, wear it with faith and venerate it with love, so that the faithful and immaculate Virgin Mother of God will protect and defend you from all harm in soul and body.

All: Amen.

Final Exhortation

Leader: Let us pray to Our Lady using the prayer recommended for daily recitation by St. Maximilian:

All: O Mary, conceived without sin, pray for us who have recourse to you, and for those who do not have recourse to you, especially for the enemies of the Holy Church and for those recommended to you.

Closing Song (optional)

Chapter Eleven

Prayers of Consecration to the Immaculata

Solemn Act of Consecration
(written by St. Maximilian Kolbe)

O Immaculata, Queen of heaven and earth, refuge of sinners and our most loving Mother, God has willed to entrust the entire order of mercy to you.

I, _____, a repentant sinner, cast myself at your feet humbly imploring you to take me with all that I am and have, wholly to yourself as your possession and property.

Please make of me, of all my powers of soul and body, of my whole life, death and eternity, whatever most pleases you. If it pleases you, use all that I am and have without reserve, wholly to accomplish what was said of you: "She will crush your head," and "You alone have destroyed all heresies in the whole world."

Let me be a fit instrument in your immaculate and merciful hands for introducing and increasing your glory to the maximum in all the many strayed and indifferent souls, and thus help extend as far as possible the blessed kingdom of the most Sacred Heart of Jesus. For wherever you enter you obtain the grace of conversion and growth in holiness, since it is through your hands that all graces come to us from the most Sacred Heart of Jesus.

Allow me to praise you, O sacred Virgin.
Give me strength against your enemies.

Babies (to be said by parents)

We greet you, O Immaculata, our life, our sweetness, and our hope.

On this day (of our son's/daughter's Baptism) we come to you as a family, to enlist your maternal love and protection.

We are especially concerned for _____'s formation as a child of God, a responsibility which lies heavily upon our shoulders.

Aware of our weaknesses and inabilities, we consecrate our child _____ to you, entrusting him/her to your Immaculate Heart and to your maternal and powerful protection.

You who are the most tender and loving Mother, the teacher of truth, the model of Christians, the unifying force of families, protect our child, whom God in his goodness has given us.

Defend _____ from evil. Make up for the defects in his/her formation. Grant us the grace to be faithful witnesses to our Faith.

Only in this way can we be at peace, knowing that you have placed _____ under your mantle until Our Lord calls him/her home. Amen.

Children

O Immaculata, turn your gaze to me. I want to live my baptismal consecration in a generous Christian life, so I can be a faithful witness to the truth. I know that I am weak and that I will experience many temptations in my life, so I consecrate myself totally to you.

In your hands I want to be a docile instrument of your love. Guide and protect me and make me fruitful in all I do, pray, and suffer.

O Immaculate Heart of Mary, accept this offering from my heart. Listen to my voice that expresses my great love for you. You are the Queen of my life, of my family, of the whole world.

Protect me as you did the Child Jesus. Keep me pure and teach me to love Jesus. Write his name on my heart with your gentle hands. Mary, be my mother for ever. I love you Mary. Amen.

Teens

I greet you, O Immaculata, my life, my sweetness, and my hope. I have come here, close to you to listen to your words of faith, hope, and comfort. Mary, it is not easy to follow Christ in the world in which I am living because it seems to judge by material success and tells me to think only of myself. There are so many temptations and I want to get rid of sin in my life. I want to love God above all else and to live in his grace. I truly desire to serve my brothers and sisters, being a witness to the Faith, even ready to offer my life for them, imitating the example of St. Maximilian Kolbe.

Aware of my weakness I consecrate myself totally to you. I know you will lead and sustain me on the path of your Son, my Savior, a path of true freedom and authentic love. In this way I can handle each day without the fear of not "making" it. Then I can live with the hope that one day there will be peace and justice on this earth.

I will not fear death knowing that you will always be at my side. Amen.

Marriage

O Immaculata, our merciful Mother, our life, our sweetness and our hope. On this day when we give praise to God because He has called us to become one, by blessing and elevating our love to a sacrament, we feel the need to turn to you. We desire that you always be at our side, guiding, directing, and sustaining us in your love.

The mission which God is entrusting to us—to walk united with each other—to be instruments of his love in the procreation and formation of children —is a special calling and will have its trials and difficulties. In times of temptation and doubt we trust you will help us to do what will please your Son, Our Lord.

We place ourselves at your feet today and consecrate our marriage to your maternal and Immaculate

Heart. In this way we are certain of obtaining the grace always to be faithful to our marriage vows, to grow in our love for each other, to accept children as a gift from God, and to become instruments of salvation in the world. Amen.

Families

O Immaculata, Queen of heaven and earth, our life, our sweetness, and our hope. On this day we the _____ family come before you to consecrate ourselves to you as your possession and property. We praise God because he has brought us together to give ourselves to you our Mother. We do this because Jesus said on the Cross, "Behold your Mother."

We need you, Mother Mary, to help us to be a truly Catholic family. Enter into our family life. Repeat to us the words you spoke at Cana, "Do whatever He tells you."

Help us to overlook one another's faults, to forgive as Jesus has forgiven us, and to love one another as Our Lord has asked us to love.

Please use our family to crush the head of the serpent. Ask your Spouse, St. Joseph, Protector of the universal Church, to keep us one in mind and heart with your Son's Vicar, Pope _____.

Today you have become the Queen of our hearts and home. May our home be a "City of the Immaculata," where the Sacred Heart of Jesus reigns for ever. Amen.

The Sick

O Immaculata, Health of the sick, Consolation of the afflicted, Refuge of sinners, I turn to your maternal and sorrowful Heart because I am in need of your help and comfort.

How often I feel the weight of my sickness and its effect upon me. My spirit, too, is weakened and I fall into depression and just want to give up. I ask God to remove this chalice of suffering from my life.

But you, Immaculata, stood at the foot of the Cross with your eyes of faith focused on Christ your Son. You knew how to join your suffering with his. You accepted suffering out of love for God and all mankind.

Teach me to be like you that my sufferings may not be wasted but rather a means of salvation for others.

I want to offer to you all my suffering in reparation for the sins which offend the heavenly Father and deny the truth.

Therefore, I _____ consecrate myself as your property and possession. Forge my powers of soul and body, my life, sufferings, death, and eternity into an acceptable offering.

United with you, Immaculata, may my sufferings become a positive means of salvation and hope. Amen.

Parishes

O Immaculata, Virgin Mother of the Church and Refuge of sinners, we join together to consecrate ourselves to your Immaculate Heart. We consecrate to you our whole being, our entire life; all that we are, all that we have, all that we love; our body, our heart, our soul.

To you we consecrate our families, our priests, (sisters, parish council, parish societies, choir, altar-boys, lectors, Eucharistic ministers, youth ministry, school children, teachers, etc.) We entrust to you the sick and the dying, the souls of the faithful departed, the entire parish family of _____. We desire that everyone may know and share in the benefits of your mission of love.

So that our consecration may be truly efficacious and persevering, and so that it may bear the fruits of a rich interior life, O Mother, today we renew our consecration as Christians and our baptismal promises.

We formally promise our fidelity to the truths of the Church with joy, humility, and firmness of will, following the teachings of our Holy Father, our Bishop, and the Magisterium of the Church.

We promise to pray the rosary, to listen to the Word of God, to obey his Commandments, to participate in the solemn feasts of the Church, to seek strength in the sacraments, especially Reconciliation and the Holy Eucharist. We pray that we may always be ready to offer our actions, prayers, and sacrifices to anticipate the triumph of the Lord's kingdom in our souls, in those of our brothers and sisters, in our parish family, and in the entire world. Amen.

O Immaculata, we consecrate ourselves to your Immaculate Heart.

Religious

Jesus, font of perfect charity, in your eternal design of love you called me to follow the way of perfection through the evangelical counsels and to be an instrument of your salvific mission.

Already through my Baptism and religious profession, I am totally consecrated to you. Yet, to live as fully as possible this pact of love with you and to live each moment in loving awareness of my calling, I also consecrate to the Immaculata all my faculties of body, mind, and soul; my life, my death, my eternity.

It was from her maternal Heart that you entered into this world and offered yourself to the Father as the victim for the salvation of mankind. Your Mother united herself with your sacrifice upon the Cross. In the spirit of reparation I wish to make an offering of my life.

O Immaculata, Mother of Jesus, Queen of virgins, welcome me into your heart, and all who are entrusted to me in the apostolate: babies, children, youth, the sick and elderly, families.

Obtain for me the graces necessary for my sanctifi-

cation and for the sanctification of all my community
so that we may respond completely to the great gift
of our vocation. Grant us a spirit of prayer and
ardent love for the Church. Bless our religious
family and grant that we and all men and women
may glorify Our Lord Jesus Christ, who with the
Father and the Holy Spirit lives and reigns for ever
and ever. Amen.

Priests

Jesus, the eternal Priest, in your design of love
you have chosen me to participate in your priesthood
for mankind's salvation and for the praise of the
heavenly Father. From my Baptism and through
the action of the Holy Spirit in my priestly ordination, I became all yours, totally and unconditionally.

In order to make reparation for my sins and the
sins of our people and for my weaknesses that hurt
my union with you, and in order to strengthen my
dedication to you, I today consecrate myself to the
Immaculata. I consecrate to her my entire being, my
spiritual life, my priestly ministry, my intellect and
will, my death and eternity.

It was from her maternal Heart that you, O Lord,
a victim of immolation for us all, presented yourself
to the Father (cf. Heb 10:5–9.) From the first moment of your Incarnation, Mary associated herself
with your mission, saying: "Behold the handmaid
of the Lord, be it done unto me according to your
word."

Therefore, O Immaculata, in a spirit of reparation and loving trust, as a priest of Christ, I offer myself to your Immaculate Heart. I am certain that with your help I will be able to carry out the priestly mission entrusted to me even in view of my fragility.

Mother of the eternal Priest, Queen of the Apostles, our hope, welcome me into your maternal Heart, rich with grace and mercy. Embrace also all those entrusted to my priestly ministry. Obtain for us the graces necessary for our sanctity, a spirit of poverty, prayer, sacrifice, zeal, purity, and ardent love for the Church and souls.

Place in my heart a pure love for God and my brethren. Grant that in you, with you, and for you I may glorify Jesus Christ, who with the Father and the Holy Spirit be given every honor and glory for ever and ever. Amen.

All

O Immaculata, our Queen and most loving Mother, to whom God has willed to entrust the entire work of our sanctification, accept this prayer of consecration.

I offer to you my whole being and my entire life, with all that I have, all that I love, all that I am: my body, my heart, and my soul.

Make me understand God's will in my life. Guide me to rediscover the gift of being a Christian in all its wonder and to know the secrets of your love. Help me to approach your beloved apostle, St.

Maximilian Kolbe, so that his doctrine and his testimony may move my will and my heart. Help me to follow in his footsteps, thereby becoming a guide to many souls and leading them to God through your Immaculate Heart. Amen.

Appendix

The monument of the Immaculata gracing the entrance to the Fr. Kolbe Missionaries of the Immaculata main house in Bologna, Italy.

The Fr. Kolbe Missionaries of the Immaculata

Origins and Growth of the Institute

The Institute of the Fr. Kolbe Missionaries of the Immaculata had its beginnings in 1954, in Bologna, Italy. We can truly say that this was one of the first fruits to emerge from the fathomless and vast Marian spirituality that Fr. Kolbe entrusted to the world.

Among those called to consecrate themselves to this new apostolic thrust in Italy was a young priest, Fr. Luigi Faccenda, O.F.M. Conv., who saw the *Militia Immaculatae* as one of the most efficacious answers to the needs of our times. Among the most faithful and committed collaborators in this Marian-missionary field there emerged in the fifties a group of young women. They, not content with offering only a portion of their time and lives to the cause of Mary, asked to be allowed to consecrate themselves to God in a more permanent way. While the world rejoiced in the first Marian Year, which celebrated the 100th anniversary of the dogma of the Immaculate Conception, the hope of this first group of women was finally realized on October 11, 1954.

Since its beginnings the Institute was blessed and encouraged by the Church through her Pastors (Cardinal Lercaro and Cardinal Poma, Archbishops of Bologna.) On August 14, 1985, the Congregation for Institutes of Consecrated Life and Societies of Apostolic Life gave the Fr. Kolbe Missionaries of the Immaculata its official recognition as a Secular Institute and definitive approval of their Constitutions.

And so another dream of St. Maximilian Kolbe became a reality: "Perhaps some day the Immaculata will want a 'City of the Immaculata' for women which is so very necessary. . . ."[1]

Its Purpose

The Fr. Kolbe Missionaries of the Immaculata is a consecrated ecclesial family which aims at achieving the perfect charity of its members and the fullness of their baptismal consecration, in order to realize in the Church and in the world a Marian, missionary, and secular presence. They profess the evangelical counsels of poverty, chastity, and obedience and strive to live the total offering of self to the Immaculata following the teachings and example of St. Maximilian Kolbe.

They fulfill their consecration to God in the ordinary conditions of the world, whether living alone, in their own families, or in groups of fraternal life. They are all equally consecrated and sent forth in order to be a leaven in the Church, in society, and in their environment. This is accomplished in a secular structure and form by the Missionary who is called to be a living presence of Mary, the consecrated lay woman, in the world.

The mission of the Institute is eminently one of evangelization and promotion of human values.

Interior Dynamism

Called to translate her consecration into apostolate, the Missionary strives to live her total offering to Christ in joy and fidelity by embracing the lifestyle which He chose for Himself, and which his Virgin Mother followed with complete dedication.

A Marian spirituality is the specific means of her sanctification. In fact, total consecration to the Immaculata allows the Missionary to realize a constant and gradual transformation of herself, in order to live a deep communion with God, the Trinity of love, with the Church, and with all men.

To attain the fullness of this ideal the Missionary seeks to cultivate a deep prayer life and an ongoing human, spiritual, and doctrinal formation.

Fraternal Communion

"Together they devoted themselves to constant prayer. There were some women in their company, and Mary, the Mother of Jesus" (Acts 1:14).

Fraternal life among the Missionaries is fostered by frequent encounters in the Houses of the Immaculata, where they seek to recreate the atmosphere of the Cenacle, living with Mary an experience of the Church in prayer, communion, and mission.

Besides being centers of spiritual formation and apostolic preparation for the Missionaries, the Houses of the Immaculata may become centers of prayer and spirituality open to all, according to their capability and the appropriateness of the undertakings.

From its very origin, the Institute has embraced and developed, with its own originality, the Marian doctrine of the Franciscan Maximilian Kolbe. The Institute is therefore closely united to the family of the Conventual Franciscan Friars.

Apostolic and Missionary Dimension

Welcoming Mary as a gift from the Redeemer, the Missionaries place themselves at the service of mankind in every environment and social class without distinction of land or nation, promoting by all means available the knowledge and veneration of Mary Immaculate. In this way they may contribute to the Christian formation of consciences and foster the return to God of those far from Him.

They collaborate in the mission of the Church, especially by means of:

— preaching the Word of God through Christian instruction, house to house evangelization, and parochial missions.

— using mass-media, especially the printed word of a Marian and formative nature, the main means of evangelization employed by St. Maximilian Kolbe.

— animating centers of prayer and spirituality, with retreats, days of recollection and study, courses in Mariology for priests, religious, and laity.

— collaborating with the *Militia Immaculatae* movement throughout the world.

Some members are witnesses to the Faith and their specific charism in the secular work world.

The Institute's Presence in the World

The Institute at the present is in Italy (where it has its headquarters in Bologna), Argentina, Bolivia, USA (California), and Luxembourg. Plans are being made to respond to the missionary appeals of other countries.

Notes

[1] St. Maximilian Kolbe, Letter, July 7, 1936, *Gli Scritti di Massimiliano Kolbe, Eroe di Oświęcim e Beato della Chiesa*, translated by Immaculata Press from material compiled and translated by Cristoforo Zambelli, 3 vols. (Florence: Città di Vita, 1976–78), 2:260.

The Volunteers
of the Immaculata

Since the beginnings of the Institute there have
been many members of the *Militia Immaculatae* movement and others who, for various reasons, were
unable to become effective members of the Institute,
but who requested to be united to it by a particular
spiritual bond.

In accordance with Canon Law which affirms
that the Institute "can associate with itself other
members of Christ's faithful who seek evangelical
perfection according to the spirit of the Institute and
who share in its mission,"[1] a new aggregate branch
of the Institute, the Volunteers of the Immaculata,
was initiated in 1988.

The Volunteers of the Immaculata participate in
the Marian-missionary spirituality of the Institute.
They choose to work for their own sanctification
and that of the world by way of total consecration to
the Immaculata in the spirit of St. Maximilian. Total
consecration in its interior dynamism and its missionary dimension unites the Missionaries and the
Volunteers into one spiritual family. Each one does

this in his or her own proper state of life and environment, resolving to live this Marian charism which is capable of forming them into both apostles and saints.

In this way they may be a true ferment in the Church, helping to bring about that unity which will be obtained only in the Heart of Mary, the Handmaid of the Lord and Mother of the living.

Volunteers of the Immaculata may be either men or women who are at least sixteen years of age. One who desires to be a Volunteer of the Immaculata may ask for more information at one of the Houses of the Immaculata.

Notes

[1] Cf. *The Code of Canon Law* in English translation (London: Collins Liturgical Publications, 1983), 725.

This book can be obtained from any of the following centers:

UNITED STATES

Fr. Kolbe Missionaries of the Immaculata
Spes Nostra MI Center
531 East Merced Avenue
West Covina, California 91790
(818) 917–0040

Marytown
National MI Center
1600 West Park Avenue
Libertyville, Illinois 60048
(708) 367–7800

Maximilian Kolbe MI Center
66 School Street
Granby, Massachusetts 01033
(413) 467–9190

Holy Cross MI Center
P.O. Box 158
Mesilla Park, New Mexico 88047

ITALY

Missionarie dell'Immacolata "P. Kolbe"
40044 Borgonuovo di Pontecchio Marconi Bologna
(051) 84.50.02 / 84.56.07

Missionarie dell'Immacolata "P. Kolbe"
Via Orazio 3
00193 Roma
(06) 68.78.907

Missionarie dell'Immacolata "P. Kolbe"
Via San Marco 70
37138 Verona
(045) 56.27.11

Missionarie dell'Immacolata "P. Kolbe"
Via Napoli 414
70123 Bari
(080) 44.44.17

Missionarie dell'Immacolata "P. Kolbe"
Casa di Esercizi
41042 Fiorano Modena
(0536) 83.02.08

Missionarie dell'Immacolata "P. Kolbe"
Via Lagarete 41
40040 Pian del Voglio Bologna
(0534) 98.225

Missionarie dell'Immacolata "P. Kolbe"
Via Carlo Cattaneo 96
20025 Legnano Milano
(0331) 54.67.98

Milizia Mariana
Piazza Malpighi 9
40123 Bologna
(051) 23.79.99

Milizia dell'Immacolata
Direzione Generale
Via San Teodoro 42
00186 Roma
(06) 679.38.28

ARGENTINA

Misioneras de la Inmaculada
CC 311
7400 Olavarria Buenos Aires
(0284) 20.997

Misioneras de la Inmaculada
CC 3
1744 Moreno Buenos Aires
(0228) 21.166

BOLIVIA

Misioneras de la Inmaculada
CC 3
Montero Santa Cruz
(092) 21.331

LUXEMBOURG

Missionnaires de l'Immaculée, P. Kolbe
Presbitére Hollerich
130, Route d'Esch
L–1471 Luxembourg

Other works by Fr. Luigi Faccenda in English, Spanish, and Italian (Available through Immaculata Press):

English

Symbiosis: Contemplation and Action

Spanish

Tiempo de María (Era Mariana), Luces y Sombras de la Mujer (C'e Donna e . . . Donna), Con María hacia el Tercer Milenio (Con Maria in Terrasanta), María, Camino de Esperanza (La Speranza del Duemila), Un Secreto para Descubrir (Alla Scoperta di un Segreto)

Italian

Il Mio Amore ha un Nome, . . . E Mi Segua, Ora Tocca a Voi, A Tu per Tu con Padre Kolbe, Tante Luci nella Notte, Sulle Strade con Maria, A Te la Mia Preghiera, Lettere a un Adolescente, 30 Problemi e un Uomo, Ascolta Ti Parla Padre Kolbe, Maria Speranza Nostra, Consolatrice degli Afflitti